Management
Support Systems

Management
Support Systems

Harry Katzan, Jr.

VNR VAN NOSTRAND REINHOLD COMPANY
NEW YORK CINCINNATI TORONTO LONDON MELBOURNE

Library of Congress Catalog Card Number: 83-10456
ISBN: 0-442-24753-2

Manufactured in the United States of America

Published by Van Nostrand Reinhold Company Inc.
135 West 50th Street
New York, New York 10020

Van Nostrand Reinhold Company Limited
Molly Millars Lane
Wokingham, Berkshire RG11 2PY, England

Van Nostrand Reinhold
480 Latrobe Street
Melbourne, Victoria 3000, Australia

Macmillan of Canada
Division of Gage Publishing Limited
164 Commander Boulevard
Agincourt, Ontario MIS 3C76, Canada

Library of Congress Cataloging in Publication Data

Katzan, Harry.
    Management support systems.

    Bibliography: p.
    Includes index.
    1. Electronic data processing—Management. I. Title.
QA76.9.M3K37   1984   658'.054   83-10456
ISBN 0-442-24753-2

Preface

A computer-based information system that supports executive, managerial, and administrative activity though informational and computational resources is called a *management support system.* This classification necessarily incorporates most concepts of decision support systems, composite information systems, office information systems, modeling/stimulation/optimization systems, and database systems. There are notable similarities and differences between each of these types of systems, and this book attempts to capture the major areas of commonality among them. Management support systems are complementary to traditional EDP/MIS systems, but there is one key distinction between them. An EDP/MIS system purports to optimize computer performance, whereas a management support system attempts to enhance managerial performance.

The term *management support systems* is proposed because more commonly used names, such as DSS for decision support system, have become buzzwords in the computer field to be exploited by aggressive computer and software vendors. But there is another important reason for the new name. Support systems are an integrated blend of management judgment and a technical foundation of computers and associated equipment, data communications facilities, database technology, and software application packages. The key elements in an effective management support system are the organizational setting and the managerial style of associated knowledge and support workers. The objective of a management support system is to enhance decision making, and a proper environment is necessary to synthesize efficient and effective results.

The subject matter of the book ranges from management style to advanced computer systems in order to support this important but diverse topic. Some of the key subject areas covered are: management style, decision support systems, support systems structure, patterns of user interaction and data flow, database concepts, relational database facilities, generic data operations, the information center concept, support systems architecture, integrated support systems, and planning for management support systems.

The book may be read and understood by persons who are not computer scientists.

It is a pleasure to acknowledge the cooperation of several persons who assisted in various ways with the project: J. Andren, L. Baerenwald, R. Bonzagni, R. Conner, S. Duch, C. Lybrook, T. Schipani, S. Sonkin, M. Subhas, S. Thompson, A. Walker, and D. Ziolkowski. My wife Margaret assisted with the preparation of the manuscript and handled the word processing; she deserves special recognition for being a good partner during the entire project.

HARRY KATZAN, JR.

Contents

Preface / v

1. **Rationale for Management Support Systems** / 1
    Introduction / 1
    Management Style / 3
    Scope of Management Support Systems / 11
    Illustrative Case Studies / 16
    Summary / 24
    Selected Reading / 26

2. **Basic Concepts for Management Support Systems** / 27
    Introduction / 27
    Basic Functions of a Management Support System / 27
    Systems Structure and Operation / 28
    Patterns of User Interaction and Data Flow / 36
    Knowledge-Based Systems / 40
    Summary / 44
    Selected Reading / 45

3. **Database Facilities for Management Support Systems** / 46
    Introduction / 46
    Systems Approach to Information Management / 47
    Database Concepts / 49
    Generic Data Operations / 54
    Relational Database Management / 71
    Summary / 80
    Selected Reading / 82

4. **Providing Management Support Services** / 83
    Introduction / 83
    Information Center Concept / 84
    Support System Architecture / 90
    Integrated Support System — A Case Study / 94

Summary   /   97
Selected Reading   /   98

5. **Strategic Planning for Management Support Systems**   /   **100**
Introduction   /   100
Strategy and Planning   /   100
Justification   /   103
Implementation   /   104
User Acceptance   /   106
Summary   /   107
Selected Reading   /   108

Bibliography   /   **109**

Index   /   **113**

Management
Support Systems

1
Rationale for Management Support Systems

INTRODUCTION

Many of the key activities in modern organizations are concerned with methods of increasing productivity. The subject is discussed by executives, managers, administrators, knowledge workers, support workers, clerical staff, and even blue-collar workers. Proposed solutions to the productivity dilemma range from participative management to automation through artificial intelligence and industrial robots. Nestled somewhere between the two extremes is the underlying belief that increased productivity is related to advance in computer technology. Notions in this regard are not unfounded since computers have in fact increased productivity to a very large degree through scientific computation, data processing, and on-line/real-time systems. Moreover, the quest for increased productivity is not limited to the working class alone. Enlightened executives, managers, and administrators have begun to look at their own activities in order to enhance personal achievement. Age-old methods of management are being challenged and subsequently placed in proper perspective.

Computer-Based Information Systems

What seems to be emerging from this realignment of management thinking is the recognition that the effective use of information in an organizational environment is fundamental to good performance — at all levels. People are talking about *decision support systems,* defined informally as computer-based information systems specifically designed to facilitate the processes of decision making. Beneath the surface, however, it appears as though the name decision support system, or DSS for short, is another one of those ever-present EDP buzzwords that essentially means whatever a salesperson wants it to mean. Other concepts that have been equated to some extent with decision support systems are: management information systems (MIS), office information systems (OIS), corporate reporting systems (CRS), and model management systems (MMS). There are probably many more acronyms that could be added to the list. Clearly, a case could be made in each and every example to demonstrate difference or similarity, as the case may be.

There is another problem with the use of the label *decision support system,* and it relates to the question of precisely what is a decision. Obviously, a purchasing clerk makes a decision upon reordering a supply of parts; but this is not exactly what most people regard as a decision. The clerk may inspect a computer-generated report before placing the order but the computer system is not referred to as a DSS. It is an information system.

To sum up, there are a lot of systems of this type that involve information, computers, reports, planning, forecasting, and so forth. Periodic reports are generated in some cases and special ad hoc reports are required in others. Similarly, unique computer programs must be constructed for some analyses, and general modeling packages can be used for other studies.

The manner in which computer-based information systems are used adds another dimension to the underlying concepts. Managers employ differing cognitive styles depending upon the problem domain and utilize information in different ways. Moreover, there is not complete agreement on what managers do.

Management Support Systems

A computer-based information system that supports executive, management, and administrative activity through informational and computational resources is called a *management support system.* This classification necessarily incorporates most aspects of decision support systems, reporting systems, office information systems, modeling/simulation/optimization systems, and database systems. It is important to recognize that management support systems involve the use of computers and associated equipment, data communications facilities, database technology, and software application packages. The last category includes, but is not limited to, financial planning and modeling packages, database query systems, reporting systems, and information management systems.

MANAGEMENT STYLE

It appears to be self-evident that management style determines to a large extent how a person views information and how effective a management support system could be in that organizational setting. For example, one executive could view the absence of information as a definite threat, while another might view the same situation as a challenge. Four relevant topics are covered: executive information space, general models of decision processes, cognitive style, and leadership styles.

Executive Information Space

In management, administration, and personal life, people view and react to their own information space in a variety of ways. In this context, a person's *information space* is the informational environment in which he or she customarily operates, and ordinarily consists of what that person knows in relation to what other people know.

This personal information space can be conceptualized through the use of a Johari window, created to model interpersonal communications. As shown in Figure 1.1, a Johari window is comprised of two axes and four quadrants. It concerns behavior, feelings, and motivation known to a person's self and to others. Thus, quadrant 1 denotes information known to the self and others and is called the *open* quadrant. A large first quadrant represents good interpersonal relations, and working with others is facilitated. Quadrant 2 represents information that is known to others but not to one's self. In Johari theory, this is the *blind* quadrant and represents a degree of vulnerability, at the interpersonal level. For example, an arrogant person may misread his or her own behavior as self-assertiveness and not recognize the extent to which others may mistrust him or her. Quadrant 3 signifies information known to one's self and not others and is known as the *hidden* quadrant. This quadrant is governed by social custom and the aspirations of the self. Since the person is effectively in charge of self-disclosure, a balance of spontaneity and discretion effectively determines the efficacy of this quadrant. Lastly, quadrant 4

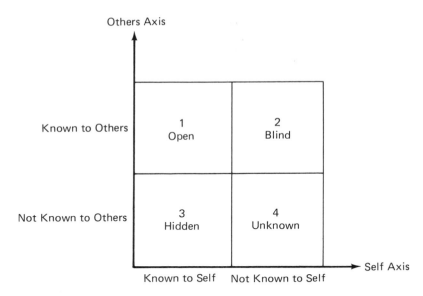

Figure 1.1 Johari window. (The name is pronounced as a combination of Joe and Harry, after its originators: Joseph Luft and Harry Ingham. See references.)

refers to information not known to the self and also to others, and is named the *unknown* area. This quadrant can represent unknown problems and untapped resources. In short, experiences and events associated with the fourth quadrant can lead to unpredicted outcomes.

In the realm of *management support systems,* the notion of Johari analysis leads to an awareness of usable information in the decision-making process. The objective, of course, is to provide as much relevant information as possible to the decision maker, and this scenario is conveniently conceptualized as a Johari model in Figure 1.2. The diagram is concerned with organizational information available through an information system, and purportedly useful in the decision-making process, and with the degree to which a decision maker is in the position to use this information in the decision-making process. Quadrant 1, arbitrarily labeled the *alpha area,* denotes information available for decision making and additionally in the possession of the decision maker in an appropriately usable form. Clearly, the objective is to make this area as large as possible so that both sound managerial judgment and relevant information serves as input to a decision resulting in effective action. The information

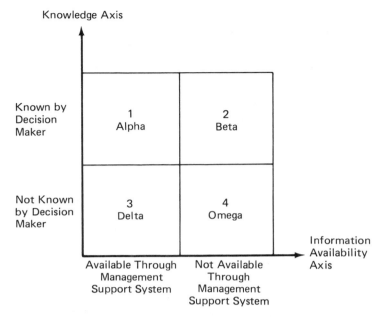

Figure 1.2 Executive information space conceptualized as a Johari model.

that affects a decision varies from case to case, but is usually drawn from three sources:

- The business environment
- Industry data
- Enterprise data

Thus, the information resource may be available from internal sources, external services, or a combination of the two.

Quadrant 2, named the *beta area,* refers to knowledge that is possessed by the decision maker but is not available from an information resource. This is judgmental information gained from experience or private sources.

Quadrant 3, called the *delta area,* represents information that is not available to the decision maker in a useful form or is outside of the domain of the decision maker. Depending upon the needs of a particular scenario, it is clearly desirable to move as much information as possible from delta to alpha.

Lastly, quadrant 4, named the *omega area,* indicates a situation where insufficient information is available to make a sound decision. The main objective in management support systems is to keep the omega area as small as possible.

The analogy between the application of Johari analysis to information space is not a perfect representation, but unmistakably leads to a distinction among various broad classes of decisions. This subject is covered in succeeding sections.

General Models of Decision Processes

Decision processes can be classified according to the types of information involved, but no decision maker can possibly handle the voluminous amounts of data relevant to even a medium-sized problem. Data must be "distilled" through analysis techniques that include composition, selection, summarization, consolidation, and transformation. In the mind of the decision maker, experience, intelligence, and intuition are combined to form judgment. Thus, distilled data and judgment are inputs to a decision, and as mentioned above, the output is the resulting action.

Decisions that involve only the information dimension are regarded as *structured decisions.* Typical examples are inventory management, manufacturing control, and some forms of financial analysis. Decisions involving the information dimension and managerial judgment are called *semistructured* decisions, and characteristically involve tasks such as tactical and financial planning, budgeting, forecasting, and project evaluation. The techniques that apply to semistructured decision making include financial modeling, risk analysis, statistical analysis, and simulation. Decisions involving judgment alone are known as *unstructured decisions* and are normally associated with strategic and long-range planning.

Computer support for structured decisions is an outgrowth of data processing and is commonly embodied in a management information system (MIS). Historically, the biggest problem with the MIS concept has been the fact that the "structured decision" approach is applied to cases where judgmental input is necessary.

Computer support for semistructured decisions is what management support systems are all about. Managerial judgment is necessary for interaction with the computer on a demand basis and for the decision process itself. The fact that computer needs cannot be completely specified in advance effectively determines the difference between management/decision support systems and traditional management information systems.

Unstructured decisions depend completely on managerial judgment and are heavily related to a manager's cognitive style. The next two sections survey this important topic because there is a growing need for support systems that enhance managerial judgment.

Information Dynamics

Most organizations function as "pseudo" information processors. Through established practices of reporting, information is summarized and abstracted for management as it flows upward. Similarly, management control and policy information is expanded and detailed for organizational use as it flows downward. This is where the so-called 80-20 rule comes from. It is estimated that 80% of the information used in a department is generated within the department and only 20% comes from outside. In an analogous fashion, 80% of the information handled by a department will be used only in that department, and 20% will be sent outside that department.

To a large extent, the filtering of information is characteristic of a hierarchy and thereby creates the necessity of having to make unstructured decisions more often than is desirable. Clearly, this is the delta area of an executive's information space and definitely a subject that can be broached by management support systems.

Cognitive Style

The thinking style of executives, managers, administrators, and other cognitive people determines how they organize information in order to achieve the awareness required for effective decision making. The scope of a decision situation is governed by how a decision maker assesses the environment for a decision. The extent of a decision maker's activities in a decision situation is further determined by a job description and one's perception of it. Diversity in the above processes leads to the identification of two managerial styles:

- The systematic manager
- The intuitive manager

Much has been written on this important subject and it is sufficient to suggest that the *systematic manager* uses *hard information* and systematic methods, whereas the *intuitive manager* tends to use *soft information* and less formal methods. Clearly, the choice of style depends on the individual, the decision situation, and perhaps one's position in the organization; most importantly, most managerial tasks require a combination of both styles.

In recent years, managerial style has been identified with the side of the brain that is predominantly used in various forms of managing. Research has determined that for most people the left hemisphere of the brain performs logical processes that have a linear order. Planning, problem solving, speaking, and reading are common examples of left-hemisphere functions. The right hemisphere of the brain operates in a simultaneous fashion on holistic and relational processes. Visual image processing and intuitive judgement are right-hemisphere functions. Well-developed right-side functions, for example, enable an executive to deal effectively with soft speculative inputs. To some extent, this direction of analysis appears to explain extensive management use of the verbal mode of communication. Clearly, speech is linear, but the total process allows managers to read facial expressions, gestures, and varying voice forms. As with managerial style, most activities involve both sides of the brain, but nevertheless, individuals prefer to use their dominant side.

Seven major tasks are identified in decision making: recognition, diagnosis, search, design, screening, evaluation/choice, and authorization. Two tasks are specifically identified with cognitive style and split-brain functioning: diagnosis of a decision situation and design of a viable solution. Both tasks involve explicit information, but in a way to synergetically combine left- and right-hemispheric processes.

Diagnosis of a decision situation relates to the perceptual process of information gathering in either a preceptive or receptive mode. A *preceptive modality* involves analyzing the relationship among data groups, filtering data, and synthesizing definitive information from available data. A *receptive modality* involves focusing on detail and stresses the completeness, consistency, and integrity of data. The disadvantages of preception and reception are obvious. With preception, important details can be overlooked, and with reception, the "gestalt" may not be recognized. The objective of the "diagnosis" task is to get the meaning of the data, and the management support system can (or should) provide the bridge between preception and reception.

Design of a viable solution refers to the processes of problem solving — sometimes known as information evaluation. A *systematic modality* involves the structuring of a problem into solvable subproblems, each with a known feasible solution. Moreover, information is utilized as it "fits the solution." In this modality, the method is the solution. An *intuitive modality* is an incremental form of problem solving wherein an individual makes an incremental move in a viable direction without assessing the total solution, because of economic, social, or political reasons. The intuitive modeling is roughly akin to satisficing and utilizes methods that can best be classified as trial and error.

Cognitive style can be assessed therefore through the two established dimensions:

- Information gathering
- Information evaluation

Each combination, such as receptive and systematic modalities, requires a unique combination of judgment and information and is related to one of the decision-making models introduced previously. A management support system must complement a decision maker's cognitive style through varying forms of modeling, statistical analysis, risk analysis, reporting, and so forth.

Leadership Styles

The leadership style assumed by an executive, manager, or administrator in dealing with people carries over to the use of management support systems for information gathering and evaluation functions. The style evidenced by most leaders can be placed into four well-known categories or a combination of them:

- Autocratic
- Bureaucratic
- Democratic
- Laissez-faire

For example, an autocratic leader who adopts systematic and preceptive modalities of cognitive style would probably favor a fixed periodic reporting system, whereas a democratic leader with interactive and receptive modalities of cognitive style may favor a specialized ad hoc reporting system. Furthermore, a centralized computer facility may be associated with autocratic and bureaucratic leadership styles, whereas a person with a laissez-faire leadership style would support a distributed computer facility.

It is important to recognize that management support systems model the organization and its people. As people change, so do the support systems. The expectations of systems analysts for acceptance of management support systems is closely attuned to the persons involved.

Knowledge and Information

One of the primary advantages of a management support system is that it allows information to be gathered and evaluated within a reasonable time frame. In fact, through the use of appropriate computer facilities, information can be processed before it is needed. It is important to recognize, however, that knowing via an information system is different from knowing through personal experience. Moreover, since processed data is frequently used for decision making through management support systems, the authentication level can be lower than necessary when raw data is used. Effectively, there is a decline in the need for firsthand information and an increase in the demand for secondhand and tenuous knowledge.

In society, a person is often a member of several decision-making units ranging from personal to professional affairs. In a similar manner, information is commonly a part of several knowledge structures, wherein information is organized to serve various purposes. Once data is processed in the context of decision making, several things may take place:

- The ownership of the resulting information changes.
- The timeliness of the information must be considered.
- The consistency and completeness of the information must be recognized.

In short, the management of information by an organization is a subject that should be investigated prior to installation of a management support system.

SCOPE OF MANAGEMENT SUPPORT SYSTEMS

A management support system enhances executive, managerial, and administrative activity through informational and computational resources. The key concept is *support,* and it is unfortunate that the basic technology has been associated with the term *decision support systems.* Systems of this type do support decisions, but they support other important activities as well. Middle managers, staff personnel, and analysts also use support systems for a variety of business functions. Accordingly, this section covers three topics: decision support systems, office information systems, and composite information systems. They are all variations on the general theme of providing computer-based management support. There is some overlap between the various concepts, as suggested by Figure 1.3. The only exception, clearly, is the office information system, which serves a complementary role to the composite information system.

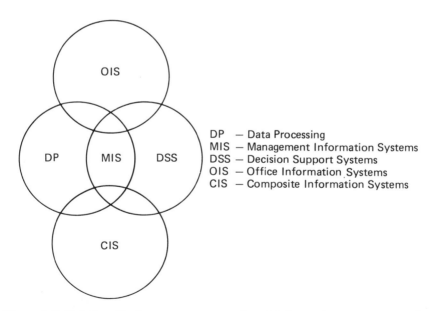

DP   — Data Processing
MIS — Management Information Systems
DSS — Decision Support Systems
OIS — Office Information Systems
CIS — Composite Information Systems

Figure 1.3 Relationship between computer-based information systems together with data processing.

Decision Support Systems

Decision support systems (also known as DSSs) are the broadest and most widely exploited type of management support system. At this stage in its development, decision support is a general concept intended to take advantage of computer-based information systems to control and enhance the ability to make effective semistructured decisions. Decision support differs from management information systems, which are designed to facilitate the making of efficient structured decisions, and from management science/operations research, which provides optimum or near optimum solutions to structured problems.

The scope of a decision support system is largely dependent upon the persons involved and the type of organizational decisions to be supported. In spite of a wide diversity of applications, it has been possible to classify support systems according to the following operational dimensions:

- *Business area,* such as manufacturing or finance
- *Decision type,* such as operational planning or financial control
- *Problem domain,* such as optimization, data analysis, or data retrieval
- *Information technology,* such as database and time-sharing

and also to the orientation of the system. In the latter category, Steven Alter* has classified decision support systems as model oriented or data oriented, according to the following hierarchy:

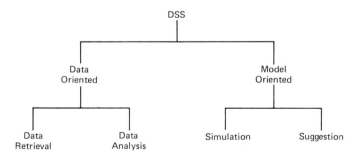

---

*Alter, S. L., *Decision Support Systems: Current Practice and Continuing Challenges,* Reading, Massachusetts. Addison-Wesley Publishing Company, 1980, p. 76ff.

Data retrieval includes query and reporting systems. *Data analysis* combines retrieval operations with statistical and financial analysis operations. *Simulation* represents accounting and representation models, and *suggestion* includes optimization and suggestion models.

There are a variety of approaches to decision support that a person can use for classification. The approach taken in subsequent chapters is to establish a set of building blocks from which support systems of all types can be synthesized.

Office Information Systems

An *office information system* is just what its name implies — a computer-based system that provides informational resources to knowledge and support workers in an office environment. An office information system is ordinarily comprised of three major functions:

- Word processing capability
- Electronic mail facilities
- Conferencing

Word processing capability refers to text preparation through the use of a computer or its equivalent. The domain of word processing includes letters, reports, documents, and other forms of correspondence. The scope of word processing also includes optical character recognition for the input of documents prepared on conventional office equipment and reprographics for output functions, which includes computer printing, copying and duplicating, addressing and packing, and various forms of platemaking and printing. Word processing works hand-in-hand with electronic mail facilities.

An *electronic mail system* is a computer-based information *and* data communication system that avoids the problem of transport delay and information availability. The scope of electronic mail includes electronic message systems, document distribution within the domain of communicating word processors, and schedule/agenda functions for managerial organization.

Conferencing is a computer-based communications technique that permits participants to engage in group interactions from remote locations. Conferencing is a blend of both old and new, since most developments are extensions of existing techniques. Major forms of conferencing are identified as:

- *Audio conferencing* – an outgrowth of the conference call
- *Communicating word processors* – storage of a document in a computer, where it is accessible to several work stations concurrently engaged in a normal telephone conversation
- *Video conferencing* – combined TV and audio facilities for remote meetings via advanced data communications
- *Computer conferencing* – asynchronous (i.e., not simultaneous) computer communications between participants without the requirement of face-to-face activity, by storing, logging, and forwarding messages and documents for independent study.

Conferencing is most frequently used for consensus decision making, training, seminars, meetings, and so forth.

Office information systems are particularly useful for management support because access if frequently permitted to a centralized database for the construction of letters, reports, and documents. The subject of office information systems, which tends to be broad, is not specifically covered here. However, the underlying technology that spans office information systems, decision support systems, and composite information systems is presented in subsequent sections.

Composite Information Systems

A *composite information system* is a member of that class of systems that extract and summarize data from conventional data processing systems, from transaction processing systems, and from external sources, and that store this information in "application" and "subject" databases for query and reporting operations. An on-line system of this type is sometimes known as a *corporate reporting system.* The term *composite* refers to the obvious fact that no data base and associated set of computational elements is strictly MIS or DSS. Thus, the scope of composite information systems can be placed between MIS and DSS, as suggested in Figure 1.4.

Applications within the domain of composite information systems are part MIS and part DSS and could realistically be placed in either category. However, these applications require computer resources

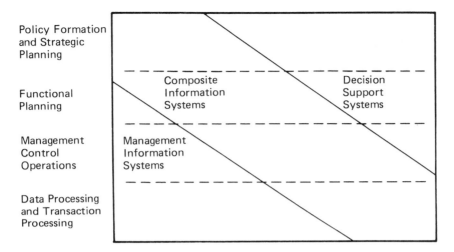

Figure 1.4 Scope of composite information systems.

and close management attention, and it is convenient to view them logically as a separate system. Clearly, a composite information system may run on the same computer resources as a transaction processing system, but is viewed conceptually as a separate entity..

Management attention is needed because end-user access to computer facilities requires special operational considerations, such as:

- Loss of integrity of transaction processing and MIS databases
- Differing levels of management data (i.e., detailed or various levels of summary form)
- Increased load on computer resources associated with interactive processing
- End-user problems, such as training, database views, and information overload

Thus, a composite information system requires special systems facilities, and how they are used depends on where an installation is coming from. For example, a file-based transaction processing system and a database-based data processing system involve different systems facilities to provide composite information system support.

ILLUSTRATIVE CASE STUDIES

A management support system is unique in the sense that is is an application of computer-based information systems to a particular organization and to unique management styles. There is no right or wrong approach. A direction that is fruitful for one organization may result in a disaster when attempted in another organization. The most important point to be remembered is that success is technology driven, and the underlying hardware and software facilities determine what can and cannot be accomplished. Even as important a subject as end-user acceptance is largely dependent on user languages, query systems, and database design. This section serves as a "window" to the underlying technology by giving representative case studies from human resources and banking.

Human Resources

In many large organizations, the management of human resources information is as significant as the management of the people themselves. In a decentralized organization, information must be managed at three levels:

- Corporate headquarters human resources planning
- Local level human resources planning
- Local personnel management systems

At the corporate headquarters level, a management support system is needed for national and worldwide policymaking, interdivisional comparison, government statistics, pension plans, salary surveys, insurance contracts, operational methods and guidelines, and a variety of other top-management needs. At the local level, a management support system is required for local policy issues, placement and promotion, hiring and firing, benefits administration, and local operational methods. Local personnel management systems could be classed as composite information systems. For example, a local personnel system would include the capability for keeping track of all benefits and claims for employees, dependents, and beneficiaries for a variety of benefit plans.

The basic objective of a human resources information system is to provide information to management on:

- What has happened in the past
- What is currently happening
- What will happen in the future

in the area of human resources planning and administration. Through effective analysis, it is also desired to provide an answer to the "why" question for each of the above "what" questions. In order to satisfy this objective, a management support system for human resources planning and administration should be able to provide information in three general categories:

- Employees (e.g., head count, types, costs, experience/skills, education/training, performance, location, organization)
- Organization (e.g., authorized strength, cost, movement, age, experience/skills)
- External factors (e.g., labor trends, sales, product planning, legislative action)

In order to provide this information, a human resources management support system would have to supply capability for data analysis, modeling and simulation, periodic and ad hoc reporting, and a means of viewing different subject databases.

Figure 1.5 gives an overview of data flow in a human resources management support system. Input from each operating division takes three forms:

- *Line department input*
  Job evaluations
  Skills
  Time
- *Personnel changes*
  Job evaluations
  Training
  Assessments
  Movements
- *Payroll change data*
  Rate
  Personal data
  Benefits and deductions

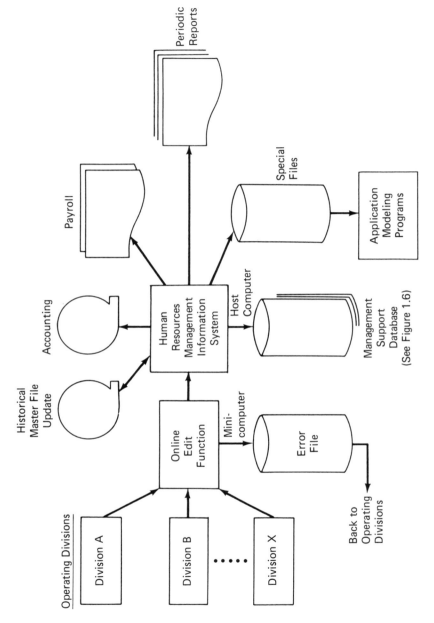

Figure 1.5 Data flow in a human resources management support system.

This data, transmitted to the human resources center on a monthly basis, is edited and passed to a human resources management information system for conventional data processing. Data not passing the edit test is returned to the operating division.

The human resources management information system performs conventional MIS/EDP processing and generates the following files and database:

- Historical master file (sequentially organized)
- Accounting file (sequentially organized)
- Payroll output
- Periodic reports
- Special files for application modeling programs
- Management support system database

The data base is used for end-user support as depicted in Figure 1.6.

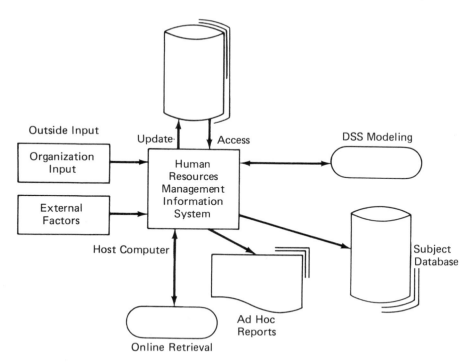

Figure 1.6 Decision support in a human resources management support system.

The human resources management support system, shown in Figure 1.6, takes organizational and external input, as covered in the preceding text, and provides the following decision support services:

- On-line retrieval
- Ad hoc reports
- DSS modeling
- Subject database

Subject databases are subsequently used for special query and modeling purposes.

The people and computer resources necessary to support the human resources system are grouped as follows:

- Operations
- Editing function
- Data administration
- Retrieval and analysis

Operations are essentially the same as conventional EDP operations. Functions performed are system scheduling, file changes and maintenance, data acquisition, system software updates, subsystem interfacing, archiving, recovery, and transmission of results.

The *editing function* involves the establishment of editing rules, data acquisition, data entry, error resolution, data transmission to a host computer, and administration of accuracy and collection procedures.

Data administration is a key function in a management support system since most activity is data driven. Primary tasks are systems changes and enhancements, data modeling, user training, database security, and administration of subject databases.

Retrieval and analysis involves end-user support and incorporates database knowledge, retrieval and query procedures, and analysis/modeling support. This category involves both effective software for retrieval and analysis, and also key people who can understand and evaluate user needs. The information center concept, covered later, is a useful mechanism for providing effective end-user support.

End-user training is problematical because of varying backgrounds. Training seminars are needed to acquaint prospective users, and the subject matter should include, but not be limited to, retrieval and analysis procedures, data organization, and the meaning (i.e., the subject matter) of the data itself.

Banking

The preceding section, covering a human resources case study, effectively establishes the underlying philosophy of a management support system. In a banking environment, it is necessary to supply service and information to both banking customers and internal bank employees. With human resources, the problem domain includes only internal employees.

A typical management support system in a banking environment might incorporate the following scenarios:

- An on-line network of customer banking/cash dispenser units
- An on-line network of teller banking terminals for customer service and other banking functions
- A large centralized computer complex that provides the following management support services:
  Conventional EDP support
  MIS for periodic reports
  Office information system access to an on-line database
  Decision support for ad hoc reporting, query, and analysis

The on-line database contains customer banking data to assist in providing on-site branch customer service.

Figure 1.7 gives an overview diagram of the on-line customer banking network. The banking/cash dispenser units are driven by minicomputers, connected by data links for the file transfer of nonlocal account data. The minicomputers have limited direct-access storage, so the minimum amount of information needed for satisfying customer demands is maintained locally. Full account data is stored in the host computer. Periodically, transaction records are written to tape and transported to the host computer, where master customer records are verified and updated. Operational customer data is then returned by tape to the local minicomputers. A conceptual view of a banking management support system is contained in Figure 1.8.

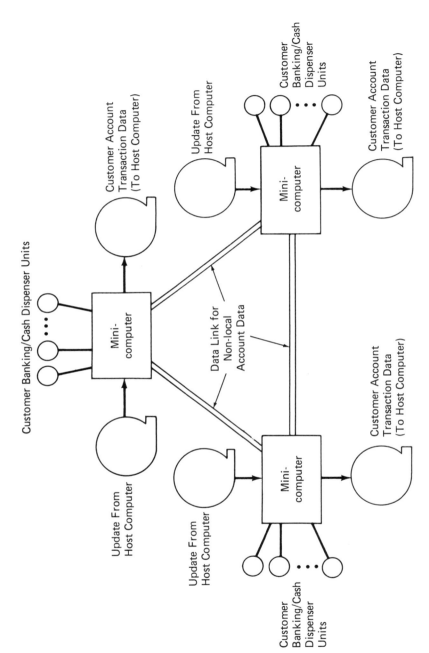

Figure 1.7 On-line network of customer banking/cash dispenser units.

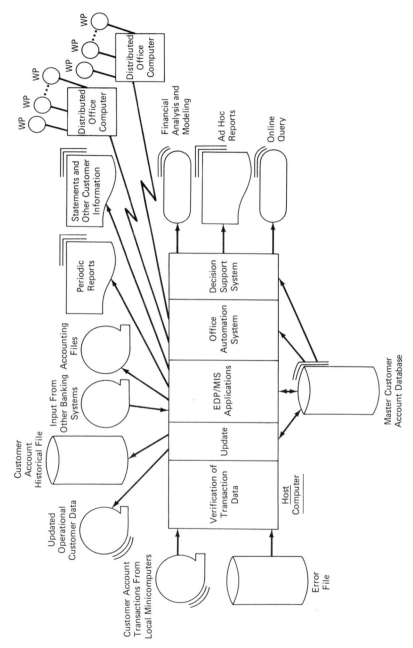

Figure 1.8 Conceptual view of a banking management support system.

A master customer account is maintained for access by EDP/MIS applications, office information systems, and decision support systems. This database is backed up as a historical file. Standard EDP/MIS applications are designed to accept input from other banking systems, such as check processing, and accounting files, periodic reports, and customer information are generated during the execution of standard EDP/MIS application programs.

An office information system composed of distributed office computers and word processing stations has access to the master customer account database for the generation of relevant letters, reports, and documents. A request for a database access is accepted by the distributed office computer and forwarded to the office information system executing out of the host computer. The host is also used as a pipeline and a repository for messages and for document storage.

The decision support system provides on-line query to the master customer account database and facilities for ad hoc reports and financial analysis and modeling.

It is important to recognize that after the verification and update runs have been completed, the master customer account database is available for use in EDP/MIS applications, in office information system service, and in decision support system facilities. In this host-based system, the database is centralized for operational reasons since it is frequently updated. If, for example, updates were infrequent, then the database could be subdivided into application and subject databases and off-loaded to other computer resources.

Because of banking security requirements, data administration is a critical function in the total management support system. Each application domain must have its own view of the data. By subdividing or off-loading, the scope of the security problem is reduced.

SUMMARY

Productivity improvement is a key activity in modern organizations, and it is currently being stressed by executives, managers, administrators, knowledge workers, support workers, clerical staff, and even blue-collar workers. A well-founded belief exists that increased productivity is related to advances in computer technology. Age-old methods of administration are being questioned.

One sure fact has emerged from this concern over productivity. It is the recognition that the effective use of information in an organization is fundamental to good performance. In this context, people are talking about decision support systems, defined informally as computer-based information systems specifically designed to facilitate the processes of decision making. For a variety of practical reasons, the name decision support systems, or DSS for short, is becoming regarded as just another EDP buzzword to be exploited by aggressive salespersons. Moreover, there are several varieties of systems that involve information, computers, reports, planning, forecasting, and so forth. Questions have also arisen concerning the nature of the decision process itself and the adaption of systems to a manager's cognitive style.

A fresh classification that encapsulates decision support and related systems is proposed. A computer-based information system that supports executive, management, and administrative activity through informational and computational resources is called a *management support system.* This classification necessarily incorporates most aspects of decision support systems, reporting systems, office information systems, modeling/simulation/optimization systems, and database systems. A management support system involves the use of computers and associated equipment, data communications facilities, database technology, and software application packages. Software application packages include, but are not limited to, financial planning and modeling packages, database query systems, reporting systems, and information management systems.

Management style determines how a person views information and how effective a management support system can be in a particular organizational setting. Important considerations are an executive's information space, types of decision (i.e., structured, semistructured, or unstructured), information dynamics, cognitive style, and leadership style. Most importantly, it is necessary to know how information is managed in an enterprise.

In any given organization, a management support system is comprised of elements from three generic system types:

- Decision support systems
- Office information systems
- Composite information systems

Each type of system has its own definitive characteristics which necessarily overlap to some degree. All are computer-based information systems with an emphasis on a particular aspect of the problem domain.

Two case studies set the stage for management support systems technology: human resources and banking. Both examples illustrate the data collection, verification, database, and interdisciplinary aspects of management support systems.

SELECTED READING

Alter, S., *Decision Support Systems: Current Practice and Continuing Challenges,* Reading, Massachusetts: Addison-Wesley Publishing Company, 1980.

Glaser, R., and Glaser, C., *Managing by Design,* Reading, Massachusetts: Addison-Wesley Publishing Company, 1981.

Harvard Business Review, *On Human Relations,* New York: Harper & Row, Publishers, 1979.

Katzan, H., *Distributed Information Systems,* Princeton: Petrocelli Books, Inc., 1979.

Katzan, H., *Multinational Computer Systems: An Introduction to Transnational Data Flow and Data Regulation,* New York: Van Nostrand Reinhold Company, 1980.

Luft, J., *Of Human Interaction,* Palo Alto, California: National Press Books, 1969.

McKenney, J. L., and Keen, P. G. W., "How Managers' Minds Work," Harvard Business Review, *On Human Relations,* New York: Harper & Row, 1949, pp. 30–47.

Mintzberg, H., "Planning on the Left Side and Managing on the Right," Harvard Business Review, *On Human Relations,* New York: Harper & Row, 1979, pp. 4–18.

Nolan, R. E., Young, R. T., and Di Sylvester, B. C., *Improving Productivity Through Advanced Office Controls,* New York: Amacom, 1980.

Rockhart, J. F., and Treacy, M. E., "The CEO Goes On-line," *Harvard Business Review,* Volume 60, Number 1 (January–February, 1982), pp. 82–88.

Sowell, T., *Knowledge and Decisions,* New York: Basic Books, Inc., 1980.

2
Basic Concepts for Management Support Systems

INTRODUCTION

A good management support system is a delicate balance between simple versus complex and between useful versus usable. What this means is that computer technology should be used to keep the user interface as simple as possible and that data must be usable to the end user and to the decision maker, if they are not the same person. It is important to emphasize, however, that the underlying computer facilities are key to an effective management support system. A system can be so simple that it is not useful for anything but trivial decisions. Certainly, there is a place for simple systems that can be learned in 15 minutes or even a few hours. The greatest impact can be gained, however, from management support systems that require some end-user training regarding procedures and information, and from computer resources with sufficiently sophisticated software to allow complex application data to be easily accessed and manipulated.

BASIC FUNCTIONS OF A MANAGEMENT SUPPORT SYSTEM

Much of the early effort in business and management schools concerning support systems for enhancing decision making centered around the process of making decisions in an organizational environment. This direction resulted in a lot of talk but in very little actual progress. More recently, research has centered around functionality, which has resulted in an increasingly wide range of products and services.

A management support system needs facilities that allow a person to access an informational resource and use it effectively. In order to support this need, a management support system must provide the following functional capabilities:*

- The functional capability of selecting data from a database
- The functional capability of aggregating data into a form useful for analysis
- The functional capability of using data for estimating parameters of probability distributions
- The functional capability of performing simulation studies
- The functional capability of solving equations with simultaneous relationships
- The functional capability of performing optimization calculations

The above functions are achieved by structuring a system so that data can be retrieved from data files or a database, applying selection and aggregation operations, in a form suitable to an application software package that can be used to apply algorithms for estimation, simulation, equation solving, and optimization.

SYSTEMS STRUCTURE AND OPERATION

The process of moving data into a position for access by a management support system is largely dependent upon where the data originates and where it is going. Six generic classifications are identified:

1. Files to database
2. Database to derived databases
3. External databases
4. Time-sharing service
5. Down loading to microsystems
6. Stand-alone microsystems

Each classification has unique properties as well as general similarity to the others.

*Blanning, R. W., "The Functions of a Decision Support System," *Information and Management,* Volume 2, Number 3, pp. 87–93.

Files to Database

In many conventional batch and transaction processing systems, data is stored in standard files for efficient access by application programs and on-line systems. In a management support environment, data from distinct files must be extracted and consolidated into application and subject databases before it can be accessed by decision support software. This classification is conceptualized in Figure 2.1.

Key elements in the diagram are the application and subject databases. An *application database* is normally associated with a set of related application programs, such as accounts receivable or purchasing. An accounts receivable database, for example, may contain information on customers, orders, prices, and so forth. Similarly, a purchasing database could contain information on parts, vendors, design, and so forth. A *subject database* contains information on a single subject, such as customers, products, vendors, or parts. There is no simple rule that governs which type of database is best. For a limited application environment, it is clearly more economical to utilize an application database. For an integrated application environment, subject databases that can be joined sometimes offer a more efficient package.

A variation to the files-to-database classification is the case wherein external files are collected to form a management support database. This variation was depicted in the human resources case study introduced previously.

Database to Derived Databases

The most common structure for data storage is the derived database concept, as suggested in Figure 2.2. An interface program is run against an application database to generate one or more derived databases. A *derived database* is obtained from a detailed application database by applying a computational algorithm that converts two or more data elements to an aggregate form, such as:

Detailed *Application Database*	*Aggregate* *Derived Database*
Domestic sales Foreign sales . . .	Total sales = Domestic sales+ Foreign sales . . .

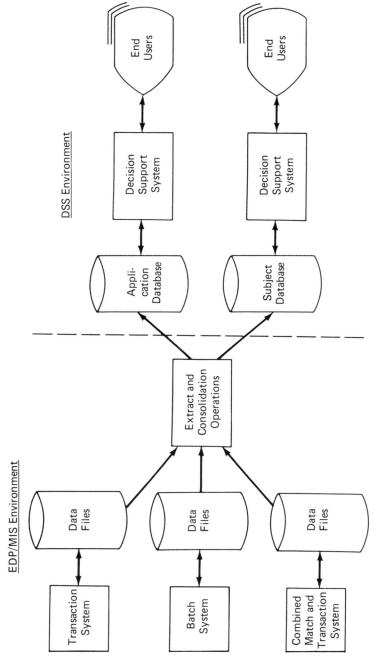

Figure 2.1   Files-to-database classification of management support system.

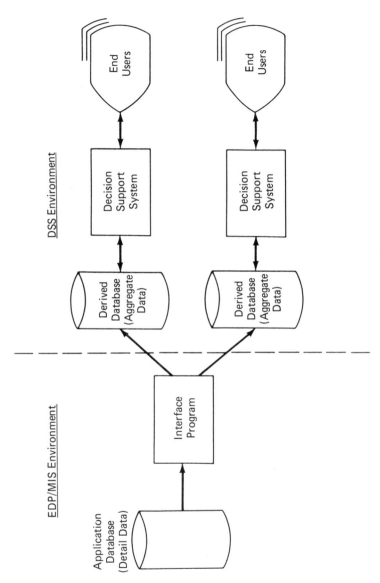

Figure 2.2 Derived database classification of management support system.

The interface program written to yield aggregate data from detailed data may additionally perform selection and consolidation operations, as well as a wide variety of additional computation operations.

External Databases

Through an on-line form of computer service, several organizations supply access to large business databases. Information obtained in this manner is useful for planning and other forms of management decision making.

The databases accessible through services of this type are typically oriented to the financial community and are generally regarded as timely and consistent, due to the specialized nature of the service. Generally classed as industry and investment databases, relevant information includes agriculture, business conditions, consumer price index, financial data, energy data, IMF balance of payments, world debt tables, and so forth.

Access to an external database is commonly combined with financial analysis and modeling capability so that the end user is provided with a self-contained decision support system. Because industry and government databases are costly to develop and maintain, they are normally used as outside services.

Time-Sharing Service

Time-sharing allows a person at a remote location to access a computer through the use of a terminal device and data communications facilities. The person is interacting with the computer as though he or she were the only user. In reality, the computer is switching rapidly between users thereby giving each the operational illusion of singleness. Actually, the computer is time-sharing.

This mode of operation permits an end user to obtain decision support service without necessarily having an in-house computer system. Through the facilities of a vendor-supplied time-sharing service, an organization can try out and then gain actual experience with a DSS financial analysis and modeling package. The organization can then migrate from vendor time-sharing service to internal computer facilities when utilization becomes high enough to justify a separate DSS computer.

In many cases, an independent time-sharing service will purchase the rights to a DSS application package as an option for their users. In this manner, an organization also can try out and gain experience with a package, as is the case when the service is being offered by the vendor of the package itself.

An outside time-sharing service is particularly useful for applications that do not require accessing external files or databases. In this circumstance, the end user enters data directly from the terminal and receives the results of an analysis or model interactively.

It is important to note that most management support services provided for the end user through internal computer facilities permit a time-sharing modality. This is a standard operating procedure. Special attention is directed to this brand of service only when it is purchased from outside vendors.

Down Loading to Microsystems

The cost, convenience, power, and versatility of microcomputers provide an alternative to one or more of the above options. The objective is to supply management support service through the use of a local microcomputer. Two options are available:

- Down load via diskette (Figure 2.3)
- Down load via data communications facilities (Figure 2.4)

When diskette is used as a transfer medium, an extract program is executed to write a diskette that is manually transported to the microsystem. The extract program accesses transaction and batch files, performs selection and aggregation operations, and physically writes a diskette, which is readable by a microcomputer under local control.

When data communications is used as a means of data transfer, the manual diskette operation is replaced by a synchronous data communications facility with appropriate software at both ends of the link. An application database interface program is mated with the extract program for selection and aggregation operations.

In the microcomputer system, aggregate data is stored on diskette for access by DSS application packages and by specially written programs. Reporting, financial analysis, and modeling capability is

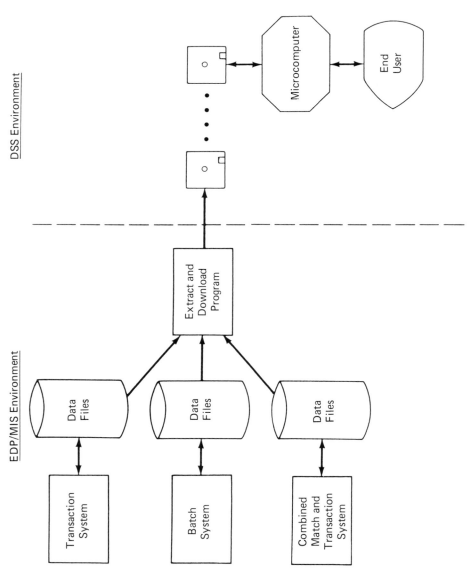

Figure 2.3   Down loading of data files via diskette to a microcomputer for DSS access.

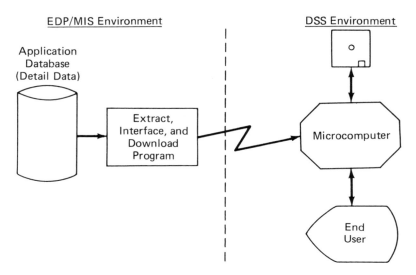

Figure 2.4 Down loading of data stored in an application database to a microcomputer via data communications facilities for DSS service.

usually available to the end user in this environment. In Figure 2.3 and 2.4, source data files are associated with a physical diskette interface and a source application database is associated with the electronic transfer of aggregate data. Clearly, there is no causal relationship between the source data and the transfer mechanism, and the methods can be interchanged.

Stand-alone Microsystems

A stand-alone microsystem has no electronic or physical diskette interface with external systems and is roughly analogous to the use of a time-sharing service. Operational data is entered directly into the microcomputer via its keyboard and is stored on diskette for access by DSS application packages and specially written programs.

Stand-alone systems are particularly applicable to departmental budgeting, estimating, data analysis, accounting, and other forms of financial analysis and modeling because of the 80-20 rule covered earlier. In some cases, however, data is taken from reports generated by host systems and is entered manually into microsystems – and time-sharing services as well. When this occurs, electronic transfer or physical diskette movement would be more effective and cost efficient.

PATTERNS OF USER INTERACTION AND DATA FLOW

At this stage in the development of management support systems and associated counterparts, such as decision support systems, the subject of exactly who uses the support system is an open question. ARmed with a couple of examples and a lot of hope, some academic people have predicted that computer terminals will be used regularly by top-management people in the reasonably near future. One of the key arguments in their favor is the contention that younger managers have been exposed to computers in most instances and this knowledge will be transferred to the executive suite. Others claim impossibility and note the quickly established distinction between knowledge workers and support workers in the area of office information systems. It is becoming increasingly clear that some top managers will get caught up in the technology of computers — especially small ones — and will use them regardless of the cost/benefit. A few others will strive to set a meaningful example for subordinates. Overall, however, it is pretty safe to assume that cost/benefit analyses will prevail and top management will be using computer terminals only if there is some definite payoff in it. This section elaborates several patterns of user interaction. The function identified as *setup* is therefore performed by a knowledge worker or a support worker, depending upon the manager's information space and the decision environment. The patterns are to be credited to Richard Monypenney,* who presented them at the DSS-82 conference in San Francisco. A basic model for interaction is given in Figure 2.5. Key elements in the process are the data, a decision maker, a decision, a setup operation, requests of various kinds, information, and computed results.

EDP/MIS Model

The EDP/MIS model does not involve explicit decisions, except those commonly regarded as structured decisions. This pattern is depicted in Figure 2.6. A request for computer service is forwarded to the setup operation that initiates a computer run and verifies the results. Periodic reporting, billing, and payroll applications — to name only a few — can be placed in this category.

---

*Moneypenney, R., "Person/Role Conflict in the DSS-Corporate Interface," *DSS-82 Transactions,* San Francisco (June 14–16, 1982), pp. 67–73.

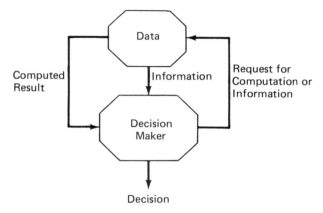

Figure 2.5 Basic interaction model.

Database Query

A database query is a request for information to assist in the making of a semistructured decision. This pattern is shown in Figure 2.7. The setup operation involves two tasks:

- Establishing a user view of the database
- Performing aggregation and consolidation operations on the data, perhaps generating a derived database

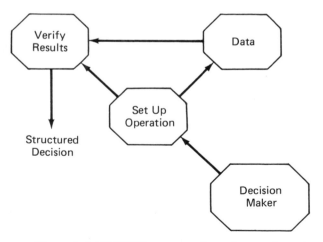

Figure 2.6 EDP/MIS pattern of user interaction.

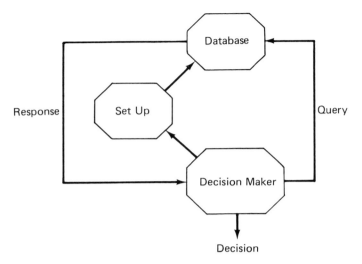

Figure 2.7 Database query pattern of user interaction.

Although the decision maker may or may not be personally accessing the derived database from a computer terminal, additional support is clearly required for data administration and for elementary decision support or composite information system operations.

Forecasting

The forecasting pattern of user interaction involves a significant computation process to do the intended forecast, as suggested in Figure 2.8. As covered previously, the setup operation prepares a derived database for end-user interaction. Input to the decision support system forecasting model constitutes the alpha area of the executive information space, consisting of three sources:

- The business environment
- Industry data
- Enterprise data

The business environment and industry data are labeled *environment data source* in the pattern. Enterprise data is obtained through a selection operation on the derived database.

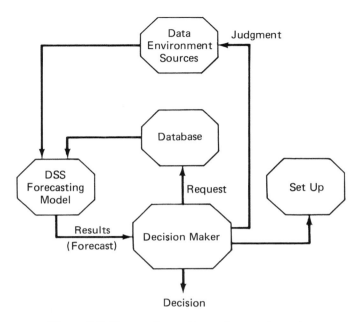

Figure 2.8 Forecasting pattern of user interaction.

The result of the computation is a forecast to be used in a semi-structured decision. Clearly, several iterations of the forecasting procedure may be required before results converge to a usable value.

Special-Purpose Decision Support

The final pattern of user interaction is the special-purpose decision support model, suggested in Figure 2.9. The key element in this pattern is the subject database used to perform "what if" analyses through a DSS financial analysis and modeling package. Typical examples in this class are portfolio planning, analysis of capital expenditures, and risk analysis modeling.

This pattern represents a generic case of an ad hoc modeling environment in which a special database can be constructed and particular computational procedures can be used to assist in making a decision or answering an important question. The true measure of an effective management support system is in its capability for supporting unique forms of analysis.

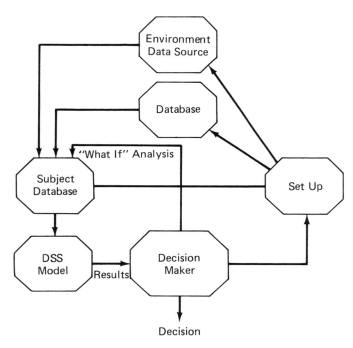

Figure 2.9 Special-purpose decision support pattern of user interaction.

KNOWLEDGE-BASED SYSTEMS

When an executive, manager, or administrator makes a successful decision, it is commonly attributed to his or her knowledge. For a manager with a systematic cognitive style, hard information and well-defined procedures are absolutely required. For a manager with an intuitive cognitive style, soft information and intuitive procedures are satisfactory. Clearly, we are referring to information in the alpha and beta areas of the executive information space; but in both cases, it must be pointed out, the emphasis is on procedures *and* information. This is what knowledge is all about.

Knowledge Representation

A database is not knowledge. Some people define information as data to which is ascribed meaning. For example, the number 25 could be a person's age or the date in the month, but it still would not be knowledge. Similarly, we say that a book is a "source" of knowledge; without an understanding reader, it is only a collection of printed pages.

Therefore, as implied at the beginning of this section, the concern is over knowledgeable behavior. Several classes of information are required for knowledgeable behavior:

* Information that represents facts about objects
* Information that represents actions and events
* Information that describes how to do things (i.e., skills)
* Information that describes information, sometimes regarded as meta-information

In general, the significance of information of this type does not depend upon whether the "intelligence" is being displayed by a person or by a computer.

Artificial Intelligence Research

Much of artificial intelligence research activity involves the design of systems that behave in a manner considered intelligent when performed by humans. The key element is reasoning and the application of the four types of information needed for knowledgeable behavior. Keen and Morton* list the areas of artificial intelligence work that are relevant to management support.

* Modeling and representation of knowledge
* Reasoning, deduction, and problem solving
* Heuristic search
* Artificial intelligence systems and languages

Some of the areas are obviously more pertinent than others. The artificial intelligence mode of thought is beginning to be transferred to other disciplines — such as management support systems — and this framework sets the stage for Alter's work, surveyed in the following section.

---

*Keen, P. G. W., and Morton, M. S. S., *Decision Support Systems: An Organization Perspective,* Reading, Massachusetts: Addison-Wesley Publishing Company, 1978, p. 40.

Framework for Support System Development

In establishing a framework for developing a decision support system, Alter* has applied the artificial intelligence mode of thought, as evidenced in the succeeding paragraphs. The basic context is that a support system is essentially a sophisticated means of answering questions and there are two parties in the process: the user and the support system. Both parties engage in two groups of activities: "thought" processes and communications operations.

On the part of the decision maker, the question-and-answer activities include:

- Deciding what to ask
- Deciding how to ask the question
- Asking the question
- Interpreting the answer
- Deciding on the next course of action

Accordingly, the support system goes through the complementary activities:

- Interpreting the question
- Selecting a method for providing the answer
- Applying the method
- Evaluating the answer
- Deciding how to report the answer
- Reporting the answer

Clearly, these activities do not reflect the support systems we have today, as reflected in Figure 2.10(a). The burden is on the decision maker to perform all of the judgmental work − even if it is trivial. What is desired is the capability of asking a question, any feasible question, and having the system provide a useful answer. Today, we need an intermediary to do this. Perhaps in the future, the judgmental work can be performed by an intermediate process, as shown in Figure 2.10(b).

---

*Alter, S., "What Do You Need to Know to Develop Your Own DSS?" *DSS-82 Transactions,* San Francisco (June 14–16, 1982), pp. 109–115.

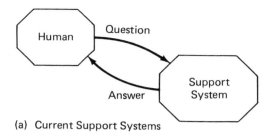

(a) Current Support Systems

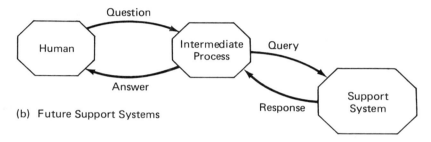

(b) Future Support Systems

Figure 2.10 Evaluation of support system capability. (a) Current support systems; (b) future support systems.

The problem lies with the substance of a question because of the potentially ambiguous nature of natural language. Alter has further identified five types of questions:

- *Factual noninferential*
  What is the sales volume for October?
- *Factual inferential*
  What would the sales volume be for October if district A were not included?
- *Instructive*
  What is the optimum production capacity of plant B?
- *Causal and inferential*
  Why has the production level of plant C fallen below the levels of other plants?
- *Predictive*
  Based on current trends, what will be our sales volume in five years?

In today's world, each of these questions could be answered in the process of making a structured, semistructured, or unstructured decision. A human intermediary is needed, however, and for several of the questions, a considerable amount of human judgment is required for interpreting the meaning of the question and for constructing an appropriate query to the support system.

On the computer end, the subject of exactly what constitutes a reasonable answer is also of interest, as are techniques for determining how to construct an appropriate answer.

These are good research topics and serve as a probable direction for future developments in the field.

SUMMARY

A good management support system is a delicate balance between simple versus complex and between useful versus usable. As much as possible, computer technology should be used to simplify the user interface and increase the usability of data.

A management support system must provide the following functional capabilities:

- Of selecting data from a database
- Of aggregating data into a form useful for analysis
- Of using data for estimating parameters of probability distributions
- Of performing simulation studies
- Of solving equations with simultaneous relationships
- Of performing optimization calculations

This capability is achieved by structuring a system so that retrieval, selection, aggregation, consolidation, and algorithmic processes can be applied to achieve the required estimation, simulation, problem solving, and optimization.

The process of providing data in a form for management support is dependent upon the origination and destination of the data. Six generic classifications are identified:

- Files to database
- Database to derived databases

- External databases;
- Time-sharing service
- Down loading to microsystems
- Stand-alone microsystems

Each classification has unique properties that effectively determine the data flow structure or use of a management support system.

The manner in which a user interacts with a support system is dependent upon the analyses to be performed and the questions to be asked. The question of exactly who will use a support system is still open. The conclusion drawn, however, is that top management will use a computer terminal only if there is some definite payoff in it. A human intermediary will probably exist to support the knowledge worker, depending upon the manager's information space and the decision environment.

Knowledge-based systems, based on artificial intelligence research, are currently being studied as future directions for support systems development. It appears as though an intermediate process can replace the intermediary between a decision maker and a decision support system, and enhance human judgment as well.

SELECTED READING

Alter, S., *Decision Support Systems: Current Practice and Continuing Challenges,* Reading, Massachusetts: Addison-Wesley Publishing Company, 1980.

Alter, S., "What Do You Need to Know to Develop Your Own DSS?" *DSS-82 Transactions,* San Francisco (June 14–16, 1982), pp. 109–115.

Barr, A., and Feigenbaum, E. A. (Editors), *The Handbook of Artificial Intelligence,* Volume 1, Los Altos, California: William Kaufmann, Inc., 1981.

Blanning, R. W., "The Functions of a Decision Support System," *Information and Management,* Volume 2, Number 3, pp. 87–93.

Cohen, C., *Composite Information Systems: Risk Factors and Implementation Strategies,* Arthur Anderson and Company, Presented at the DSS-82 Conference, San Francisco, 1982.

DSS-82 Transactions (Gary W. Dickson, Editor), San Francisco (June 14–16, 1982).

Keen, P. G. W., and Morton, M. S. S., *Decision Support Systems: An Organizational Perspective,* Reading, Massachusetts: Addison-Wesley Publishing Company, 1978.

Martin, J., *An End-User's Guide to Data Base,* Englewood Cliffs, New Jersey: Prentice-Hall, Inc., 1981.

Monypenney, R., "Person/Role Conflict in the DSS-Corporate Interface," *DSS-82 Transactions* (June 14–16, 1982), pp. 67–73.

3
Database Facilities for Management Support Systems

INTRODUCTION

As a society, we have information overload. We are practically submerged in information, but we are notably inept at using it effectively. The information we speak of is inherent in the design of buildings and automobiles, the structure of organizations, and the operations of groups and teams. As a simple example, we can receive secondary information regarding automobile design by observing existing products and imputing that choices were in fact evaluated by the manufacturer and that the best alternative for a given decision environment was selected. Other forms of information are in the printed word, recorded sound, displayed images, and so forth. Information as a subject has properties that allow us to evaluate how useful it is. These properties deal with the quantity of information and whether or not it is up to date — that is, its quality. Some factors that describe the quantity of information are its volume, its completeness, and its accessibility. Clearly, information must be usable to be useful. Similarly, some factors that describe the quality of information are timeliness, relevance, accuracy, reliability, and flexibility. We also have a tremendous appetite for information, and a lot of it is needed to operate the sophisticated everyday systems we have synthesized. The key is to manage information efficiently and effectively so that it does not become a burden to us. Information is an asset, but it can easily become a liability if it is not managed properly.

Recorded Information

Yet, as we all know by now, information becomes useful in a computer environment only when it is recorded on a medium or displayed in a form that makes it accessible to a computer. We then call it data. Ingenious methods have been developed for getting data into the computer, but getting it out is and has been a recurring problem. Traditional EDP/MIS systems are reasonably good at handling preplanned transactions — such as those in on-line banking operations — and generating periodic reports. It should be emphasized, however, that many of these EDP/MIS applications and associated procedures take many months to plan, a longer time to design, and sometimes years to implement. This is hardly a management support environment.

Data and Software Needs

What we need, therefore, to fully support the decision maker is an accessible repository of data, organized in a useful and usable manner, and an equally usable software facility for referencing the data for ad hoc reporting, analysis, and for input to decision support systems, office information systems, and composite information systems.

In short, we are calling for a database facility that is appropriate for the diverse needs of knowledge workers and support workers.

SYSTEMS APPROACH TO INFORMATION MANAGEMENT

The study of the existence of systems — called *systems ontology* — distinguishes between real, conceptual, and abstract systems. In this context, a *system* is a collection of entities — sometimes regarded simply as objects — with relationships between these entities and their attributes. The entities are the components of the system and can in general take practically any form. For example, an item of data in a database and an end user collectively constitute a system because a relationship must exist or be established to permit the user to access the data.

Systems Structure

The entities of which a system is synthesized give a system its structure and effectively delimit its functional capability. Attributes, such as the color of an automobile or the expiration date of an insurance policy, are properties of entities, and are usually associated with data stored in a database facility.

Relationships tie the entities of a system together so it can be regarded as a single unit. The relationships can take the form of a physical connection, a logical similarity, a causal rule, and so forth. In a database environment, relationships are used to associate data items to form data aggregates.

Systems Environment

The objects outside of a system are its *environment*. The manner in which the attributes of the objects affect the behavior of the system determines the class of system it is.

In most cases a system exists with the support of its environment, which is necessary for the existence of the system. Open systems interact with their environment during operation and closed systems do not. In the domain of management support, a structured decision uses closed systems thinking, while a semistructured decision uses open systems thinking.

Systems Classification

The distinction between real, conceptual, and abstract systems has relevance for management support systems. A *real system* exists independently of the observer and its existence can be perceived or inferred from observation. A *conceptual system* uses logical or mathematical concepts to model a real system's structure or operation. It is always possible to map the entities and attributes of a conceptual system into the entities and attributes of a real system. An *abstract system* is based on hypothetical/deductive arguments and has no real counterpart.

One of the major objectives of management support systems is to provide the end user a conceptual model of data that can be efficiently and effectively used to support varying forms of decision making and other diverse management activities. A conceptual model of data is in alignment with human thought processes, so a decision maker does not have to think in terms of computerized data structures. Computer software is employed to map the conceptual model of data into its real counterpart for access and for data operations.

DATABASE CONCEPTS

It is useful to look at the world of information from the viewpoint of database technology without getting swamped with the myriad details of actual database systems or even conceptual models of database systems. This section develops the concept of a *data space* and relates it to database technology.

Database Basics

A *database* is a centralized collection of data stored for one or more computer applications. This definition will be expanded in a later section. Two considerations in a database environment are of primary concern:

- The nature of data itself
- How a database must be structured to represent the existing data relationships in an enterprise

In order to properly dispose of these considerations, it is necessary to explore the fundamental properties of recorded data.

An enterprise is a collection of people and artifacts, organized to serve a well-defined purpose. An enterprise can be a business, a school, a government, a religious organization, or any of a broad class of social groups. Events take place in the course of everyday life of an enterprise that must be recorded. Since events must be stored symbolically, a data item is created, replaced, or altered to symbolically represent the occurrence of that event.

Entities

An *entity* is something about which we record operational data. An entity can be a person, place, or thing. An entity may be real or abstract.

A unit of *operational data* is simply a fact, as in the assertion: "Employee with social security number 987-65-4321 has the job title vice president." In this illustrative example, "employee" is the entity, and "job title" is a property of the entity. The property — or *attribute* as it usually called — is something that effectively describes the entity. The title "vice president" is the value of the property and is a fact recorded symbolically about the entity "employee."

In database technology, properties can also be entities about which facts are recorded. For the property "job title," we might record salary range, qualifications, and so forth. The value of a property is simply a characteristic that may apply to more than one entity. A common example of this exists when a person is one man's wife and another man's mother.

Entity Set

A collection of entities that have the same properties — but not necessarily property values — is called an *entity set.* A set of part number, policy numbers, employees, bank accounts, and dependents are all typical examples of entity sets. The entities that comprise an entity set always possess at least one unique property that differentiates among them. A unique property of this type is called an *identifier* (also called a *primary key,* as covered later). The entities in a payroll application, for example, would be employees, with social security numbers as identifiers.

Entity/Attribute/Value Space

The preceding discussion has centered around three related but different concepts: the real world, information, and data. In the real world, we customarily refer to things, properties, and real values. In the database — or the information — world, we speak of entities, attributes, and symbolic values. In the world of physical data storage, we refer to data elements and data items. Here, we are concerned with the database world. Thus, to record the fact that an entity has a specific characteristic involves establishing an attribute class and assigning a value to that attribute for the specific entity in question.

The entire notion of information in a database environment can be reduced to the three concepts presented so far: entities, attributes, and values. Clearly, an entity can possess several attributes, termed its *attribute set.* An entity set, then, is a collection of entities with the same attribute set.

A specific entity is determined through specific values for its attribute set, and an attribute/value pair is called a *descriptor.* Thus, an entity is uniquely specified by its descriptors. Because each entity stored in a database has a unique identifier, descriptors need not be unique. In fact, it is common to have different entities with the same descriptor.

Consider the following descriptors for an insurance policy entity:

Attribute	*Value*
Policy number	98765
Name	Richad Smith
Policy class	Automobile
Policy type	Liability
Policy value	1000000

Obviously, there are many other descriptors that would apply. Note that the policy number is the identifier.

Each descriptor is a fact (i.e., and element of information) that can be conveniently depicted in a three-dimensional space, where the axes represent the entity set, the attribute set, and the value set. (See Figure 3.1.) The intersection of entity plane, an attribute plane,

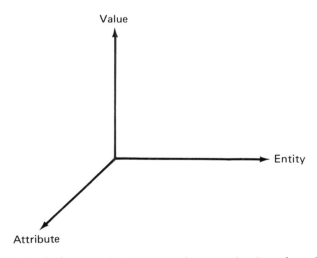

Figure 3.1 A single fact can be represented as a point in a three-dimensional space, where the axes are (1) the entity about which information is represented; (2) the attribute used to describe the entry; and (3) the value of the attribute.

and a value plane determines a fact, which is called a data element in Figure 3.2. As an example, Figure 3.2 shows the following information:

Entity:	Insurance policy
Attribute:	Policy number
Value:	98765

The entity plane runs parallel to the attribute and value axes and represents all of the descriptors for that entity.

The entity/attribute/value space conceptually represents all possible triplets of the form (<entity>, <attribute>, <value>), and is not a practical means of exposition. It does purport to give an intuitive feeling for the scope of the database problem and the reason other methods of data organization are necessary.

Database Management

A subset of the points in the total entity/attribute/value space is a *database,* which must be established and defined for a given enterprise and application set in two ways:

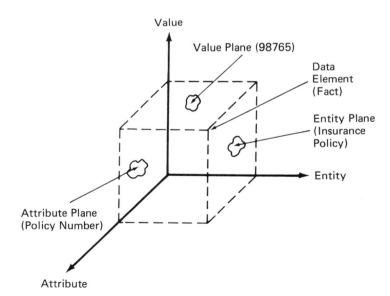

Figure 3.2 The intersection of entity, attribute, and value planes determines a fact. In this case, insurance policy is the entity; policy number is the attribute; and 98765 is the value.

- A logical description of the data in the database
- A coded form of this logical description known as the *schema*

The logical description of the data in the database allows the user to access the data interactively or via batch processing programs. The *schema* is a coded form of a logical description that allows the computer system to perform the correct accesses when a user requests an item of data.

A database management system (DBMS) is a software system that permits a database to be utilized through the interaction of software, hardware, and appropriate procedures. An overview diagram of a DBMS is given in Figure 3.3, and the key components are summarized as follows:

- A *Database description language* (DBDL), which is employed by a "database administrator" and by users to define data relationships
- A *database manager,* which is a set of software programs that interpret user commands, correspond user requests with data definitions, and make requests to the access routines for storage and retrieval operations
- A *Database command language* (DBCL), which is a set of language conventions and operational rules for using a database

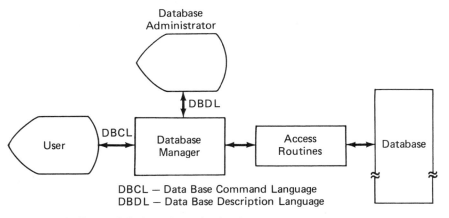

Figure 3.3 Overview of a database management system.

- *Access routines,* which serve as a physical and operational interface between the database and the database manager for storage and retrieval
- The *database,* which is the data repository, as discussed above.

The *database administrator* (DBA) is a person empowered to describe data, define relationships, define mappings, establish security precautions, and monitor performance measurement. From a management support viewpoint, the most relevant DBA function is to establish views of the database for the various user groups with the basic objective of erecting logical fences around the group's data domain, thereby obscuring this data from unauthorized users. In sophisticated systems, the database administrator, or his or her counterpart in a management support group, establishes and controls mappings from a conceptual data model to a data structure with an entirely different storage philosophy. Thus, a database designed to provide effective and efficient access for EDP/MIS applications can be viewed as a logical database that lends itself to management support applications.

GENERIC DATA OPERATIONS*

A generic data operation is a system or computational function that is representative of a wide range of different system types and software packages. A generic data operation is logical in the sense that it must be mapped into a real system before it can be executed. This section covers some basic concepts and then surveys a collection of generic data operations that are useful in a management support environment.

Data Structures

From the viewpoint of management support and computer processing, the *field* is the smallest unit of data that would lose its meaning if broken down further, and can represent one of three types of data:

---

*The generic support language used in this section is patterned after that which is available with the EXPRESS decision support system. Whenever convenient or appropriate, however, language features have been judiciously modified or extended to suit the purposes of the surrounding textual material. The information is included only for exposition purposes and should not be interpreted as instructional material on EXPRESS or any of its facilities.

- A numeric value
- Textual information
- A logical true or false value

A numeric value could be a person's age or salary, a part number, or an order quantity. Textual information could be a person's name or address, a part name, or any other descriptive information, such as a month name. A logical value is either true or false and could represent the occurrence of an event or be an indication of a condition.

Fields are grouped to form a *record;* in most cases, the fields are related as in a payroll, personnel, or sales record. The definition is completely independent of how and where the data is stored. For example, a record could be held in the random-access memory (RAM) of the computer or reside on magnetic disk or tape.

A group of related records is known as a *data file* — or simply *file* for short. Records in a file can be stored for sequential access or for direct access. With sequential access, records must be accessed in the physical order in which they were written, whereas for direct access, records may be accessed in any order. Files are normally stored on magnetic tape or magnetic disk and accessed when needed. With magnetic tape, records can only be accessed sequentially. With magnetic disk, records may be accessed sequentially or randomly, but this depends on how they were originally set up. Figure 3.4 gives a data file for a customer "order" application. The data is sorted by product code. This file will be discussed and used in later paragraphs.

A single item of data, such as a numeric value, is known as a *scalar.* A scalar value has a single component and can be used to represent such diverse items of information as a person's age and the name of a commodity. A collection of homogeneous data (i.e., data with the same attributes) is called an *array.* Only the entire array is given a name, and a particular element is selected by a subscript. A linear sequence of data items is known as a *linear array,* as shown in Figure 3.5 for a table named SALES. The concept is easily extended to two dimensions, called a *matrix,* and also to *n* dimensions. It is difficult to visualize more than three dimensions, but nevertheless multidimensional arrays have practical uses in computer applications. Figure 3.6 depicts an example of a linear array that is extended to two dimensions. In the linear array, the subscript name refers to "product" and its values are the various kinds of beverages. In the

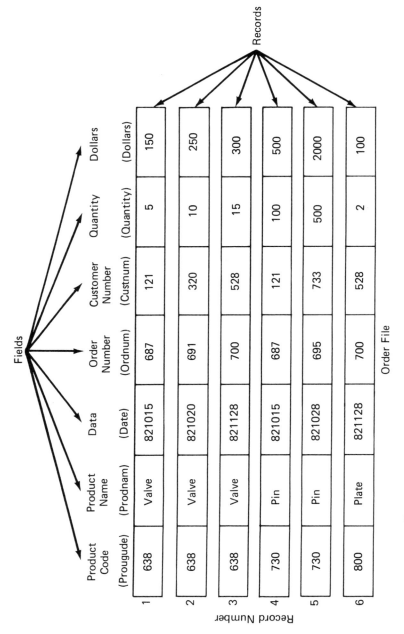

Figure 3.4 A data file sorted by product code. (Field names are in parentheses.)

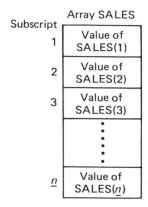

Figure 3.5 Linear array.

two-dimensional array, the subscript names are "product" and "month," respectively, and refer to beverages and the months January through December. Depending upon the software facilities available, the subscripts could be "subscript value names" or numerical indices.

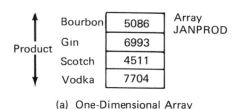

(a) One-Dimensional Array

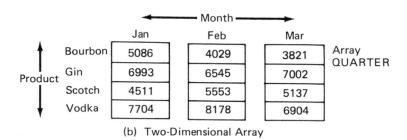

(b) Two-Dimensional Array

Figure 3.6 Extension of a linear array (a), to two dimensions (b).

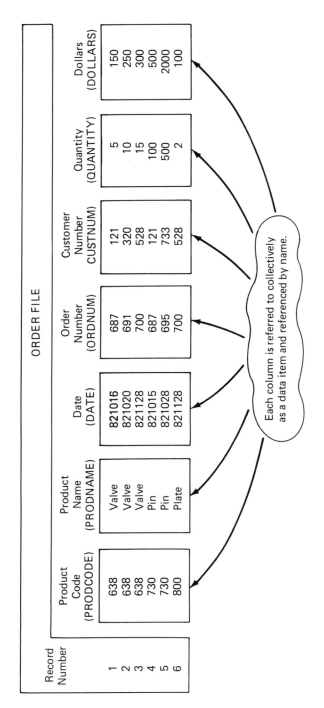

Figure 3.7 View of a data file as a set of separate data items.

Management support systems permit the end user to view a collection of nonhomogeneous data items to be viewed as an array, as in Figure 3.4 where the product name column is textual information. The "user view" is one thing, but the actual storage of data is quite another. Most software systems do in fact regard a two-dimensional nonhomogeneous "user" array as columns of independent homogeneous data items internal to the computer.

Files are *external* data structures; they reside on a storage medium external to the computer. Scalars and arrays are *internal* data structures, because storage internal to the computer, that is, random-access memory (RAM), is used to hold data during processing. Actually, the user may view an array structure as internal to the computer even though it may spill over to an external storage medium.

File Operations

One key advantage of file operations is that a sequential file written by one computer system can be transferred to another computer system for access by a management support system — in this instance, a decision support system, composite information system, or database system.

One means of viewing a sequential data file is to regard each field as a linear array extending throughout the file, as shown in the ORDER file in Figure 3.7. An associated file is the CUSTOMER file (Figure 3.8) where the "link" item is the field "customer number."

Record Number	CUSTOMER FILE		
	Customer Number (CUSTNUM)	Customer Name (CUSTNAME)	Location (LOCATION)
1	121	ACE ALUM	CHICAGO
2	320	GOOD STEEL	DETROIT
3	528	ALPHA MFG	ATLANTA
4	733	FASTENERS, INC.	HOBOKEN

Figure 3.8 A customer file related to the ORDER file (Figure 3.7) by the "link" field "customer number."

A basic file operation is to *consolidate* the two files, yielding the "consolidated" file in Figure 3.9. Two files joined in this manner can be used as a single file, thereby reducing the redundancy inherent in two separate and complete files. Operations such as consolidation are available through software facilities of a management support system. Other representative operations are selection, creation, aggregation, and simple computations.

With the latter operations, it is necessary to execute (or perform) three functions:

- Specify the file.
- Give the conditions.
- Select the appropriate fields.

For example, assume that it is necessary to select individual product orders for dollar values greater than $250 from the ORDER file and display product code, product name, order number, and dollars. The following set of generic commands would do the job:*

> USING ORDER
> LIMIT ORDER TO DOLLARS GT 250
> DISPLAY PRODCODE, PRODNAME, AND ORDNUM

ORDER	PRODCODE	PRODNAME	ORDNUM
3	638	VALVE	700
4	730	PIN	687
5	730	PIN	695

In this case, records with dollar (DOLLARS) values greater than (GT) $250 were selected, and only the product code (PRODCODE), product name (PRODNAME), and order number (ORDNUM) fields were listed. This is an example of *selection*. Note that the record number with the file name (ORDER) as a column heading is printed for reference in some systems.

Within the scope of file operations, *creation* refers to the task of creating a new file from an existing file, allowing selection, aggregation, and computation operations to be performed in the process. Suppose a

---

*The symbol > denotes user input; normally, computer output follows directly.

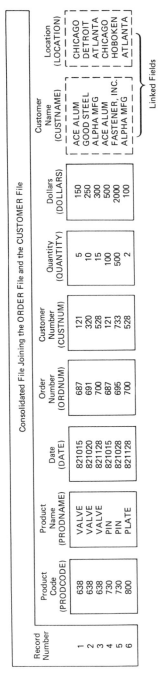

Figure 3.9 Consolidated file.

new file were needed that would contain only product code, product name, quantity, and dollars. The following set of generic operations would do the job:

```
>   USING ORDER
>   LIMIT ORDER TO ALL
>   CREATEFILE PRODUCT FROM ORDER CONTAINING PRODCODE,
    PRODNAME, QUANTITY, AND DOLLARS
>   USING PRODUCT
>   DISPLAY PRODUCT
```

PRODUCT	PRODCODE	PRODNAME	QUANTITY	DOLLARS
1	638	VALVE	5	150
2	638	VALVE	10	250
3	638	VALVE	10	300
4	730	PIN	100	500
5	730	PIN	500	2000
6	800	PLATE	2	100

In this example, a new file named PRODUCT and composed of columns product code (PRODCODE), product name (PRODNAME), quantity (QUANTITY), and dollars (DOLLARS) is created. The LIMIT statement is used to "undo" the effect of the previous LIMIT statement.

In files ORDER and PRODUCT, the product codes and product names within the records are not unique, because clearly more than one order was placed for the same product. Suppose it is desired to "total up" the quantity and dollar amounts for each product. This can be done either through the DISPLAY command or the CREATE-FILE command. The following set of commands will *aggregate* the quantity and dollar amounts for each product, creating a new file in the process:

```
>   USING ORDER
>   CREATEFILE ORDSUM FROM ORDER BY PRODCODE AND
    PRODNAME CONTAINING QUANTITY AND DOLLARS
>   USING ORDSUM
>   DISPLAY ORDSUM
```

ORDSUM	PRODCODE	PRODNAME	QUANTITY	DOLLARS
1	638	VALVE	30	700
2	730	PIN	600	2500
3	800	PLATE	2	100

DATABASE FACILITIES FOR MANAGEMENT SUPPORT SYSTEMS 63

In this case product code (PRODCODE) and product name (PROD-NAME) are used as the "break" fields to perform the aggregation, and the values for quantity (QUANTITY) and dollars (DOLLARS) are simply totaled for each set of key fields. Aggregation can also be performed by the DISPLAY command without creating a new file. In the following example, the dollar amounts of each customer order are subtotaled:

```
>  SORT ORDER BY ORDNUM AND DATE
>  DISPLAY SUBTOTAL BY ORDNUM AND DATE GIVING DOLLARS
```

ORDNUM		DATE	DOLLARS
	687	821015	150
			500
TOTAL			650
	691	821020	250
TOTAL			250
	695	821028	2000
TOTAL			2000
	700	821128	300
			100
TOTAL			400

In this case, the SORT command sorts the data by order number (ORDNUM) and date (DATE), and the form of the DISPLAY command prints detail copy and performs the "subtotal" function.

Clearly, computational operations on file data in a management support system can take a variety of forms, ranging from straight-forward column-by-column arithmetic operations to mathematical functions and DSS modeling. The following commands use the order sum (ORDSUM) files and compute the unit price based on aggregated quantities and dollars. The DISPLAY additionally contains an expression that causes the column-by-column operation to be executed:

```
>  USING ORDSUM
>  DISPLAY PRODCODE, PRODNAME, DOLLARS, QUANTITY,
   DOLLARS/QUANTITY
```

ORDSUM	PRODCODE	PRODNAME	DOLLARS	QUANTITY	DOLLARS/ QUANTITY
1	638	VALUE	700	30	23.33
2	730	PIN	2500	600	4.17
3	800	PLATE	100	2	50

The same example using a title for "unit price" and two places to the right of the decimal point is given as follows:

```
> USING ORDSUM
> DISPLAY PRODCODE, PRODNAME, DOLLARS, QUANTITY, TITLE
  "UN PRICE," 2 DECIMAL PLACES, DOLLARS/QUANTITY
```

ORDSUM	PRODCODE	PRODNAME	DOLLARS	QUANTITY	UN PRICE
1	638	VALUE	700	30	23.33
2	730	PIN	2500	600	4.17
3	800	PLATE	100	2	50.00

The expression DOLLARS/QUANTITY in the DISPLAY statements denotes that the data items in the DOLLARS column should be divided by corresponding entries in the QUANTITY column.

In spite of the versatility of file operations in management support systems, the use of array data provides a more powerful and convenient resource. The conversion process from file data to array data is a standard feature among systems of this type, and the capability of using "subscript value names" instead of numeric indices adds to the ease with which an end user can learn to use a support system of this type.

Array Operations

Generic array operations parallel file operations without the problem of dealing with cumbersome and less efficient record structures. Array data structures are known as array variables, or simply *variables* for short. Because variables are in general known to the support system, they may be used directly, as in the following example that displays a linear array (see Figure 3.6):

```
> DISPLAY JANPROD
```

PRODUCT	JANPROD
BOURBON	5086
GIN	6993
SCOTCH	4511
VODKA	7704

In this case, JANPROD is the variable, PRODUCT is the subscript name, and the labels of BOURBON through VODKA are called subscript value names.

Two-dimensional variables can be in "natural form" or as a spreadsheet. In *natural form,* variable QUARTER in Figure 3.6 would be printed as:

```
>   DISPLAY QUARTER
    PRODUCT       MONTH        QUARTER

    BOURBON       JAN              5086
                  FEB              4029
                  MAR              3821
    GIN           JAN              6993
                  FEB              6545
                  MAR              7002
    SCOTCH        JAN              4511
                  FEB              5553
                  MAR              5137
    VODKA         JAN              7704
                  FEB              8178
                  MAR              6904
```

In *spreadsheet form,* QUARTER would be printed as:

```
>   DISPLAY QUARTER BY MONTH
              . . . . . . . . . . . . MONTH . . . . . . . . . . . .
                   JAN            FEB            MAR
    PRODUCT      QUARTER        QUARTER        QUARTER

    BOURBON        5086           4029           3821
    GIN            6993           6545           7002
    SCOTCH         4511           5553           5137
    VODKA          7704           8178           6904
```

Arrays are in general a more tractable storage technique than files and provide more options to the end user.

Selection is performed by specifying a list of subscript value names, a range of subscript values, or a conditional test. The following example applies the selection operation to the linear array JANPROD with a list of subscript value names:

```
>   LIMIT PRODUCT TO GIN AND VODKA
>   DISPLAY JANPROD
    PRODUCT       JANPROD

GIN                6993
VODKA              7704
```

It should be noted here that selection pertains to a subscript, and in this case, the subscript value names of GIN and VODKA were specified. When selection is specified as a range, for example, GIN TO VODKA, the limits and intervening values are used for selection, as in the following example involving a two-dimensional array:

```
>   LIMIT PRODUCT TO GIN AND VODKA
>   LIMIT MONTH TO JAN AND MAR
>   DISPLAY QUARTER
    PRODUCT       MONTH        QUARTER

GIN               JAN              6993
                  MAR              7002
SCOTCH            JAN              4511
                  MAR              5137
VODKA             JAN              7704
                  MAR              6904
```

When selection is applied to n-dimensional arrays, only subscripts to which selection should be applied need be considered. Other subscripts assume their full range, as in:

```
>   LIMIT PRODUCT TO BOURBON
>   LIMIT MONTH TO ALL
>   DISPLAY QUARTER BY MONTH
```

	. . . . MONTH		
	JAN	FEB	MAR
PRODUCT	QUARTER	QUARTER	QUARTER
BOURBON	5086	4029	3821

The command that reads "LIMIT MONTH TO ALL" simply undoes the affect of a previous statement. Conditional tests apply to values contained in the array, as in the following case:

```
>   LIMIT PRODUCT TO JANPROD GT 6000
>   DISPLAY JANPROD
```

PRODUCT	JANPROD
GIN	6993
VODKA	7704

In this example, only those subscript values are selected wherein the corresponding element of the array has a value greater than (GT) the numeric value 6000.

Arithmetic expressions for array operations take the same form as with file operations. In the following example, an expression is used in a display statement to generate a table of production figures and a forecast reflecting 100% increase:

```
>   DISPLAY JANPROD AND JANPROD*2
```

PRODUCT	JANPROD	JANPROD *2
BOURBON	5086	10172
GIN	6993	13986
SCOTCH	4511	9022
VODKA	7704	15408

The concept applies equally well to two-dimensional arrays in natural form:

```
>   LIMIT PRODUCT TO BOURBON AND SCOTCH
>   LIMIT MONTH TO JAN AND FEB
>   DISPLAY QUARTER AND QUARTER*2
```

PRODUCT	MONTH	QUARTER	QUARTER *2
BOURBON	JAN	5086	10172
	FEB	4029	8058
SCOTCH	JAN	4511	9022
	FEB	5553	11106

and in spreadsheet form, as in:

```
>   DISPLAY QUARTER BY MONTH AND QUARTER*2 BY MONTH
              . . . . . . . . . . . . . . . . . MONTH . . . . . . . . . . . . . . . . .
                                                   JAN              FEB
                         JAN              FEB       QUARTER          QUARTER
    PRODUCT      QUARTER          QUARTER   *2               *2
    BOURBON          5086             4029         10172             8058
    SCOTCH           4511             5553          9022            11106
```

In the above examples, the symbol * denotes multiplication.

An array can be established in three ways:

- By declaration and direct assignment of values
- By the reading in of a file
- By creation of an array through the use of an expression

Only the last case is covered here. When an array is created through the use of an expression, the new variable name and the array expression from which it is to be derived must be given, as in the following example:

```
>   LIMIT PRODUCT TO GIN AND SCOTCH
>   CREATE SUBJAN FROM JANPROD
>   DISPLAY SUBJAN
    PRODUCT        SUBJAN
    GIN                6993
    SCOTCH             4511
```

In this case, a subset of array JANPROD is selected and a new array named SUBJAN is created. Clearly, the dimension and subscript values of the new array were picked up from the selected elements. A similar concept applies to high-dimensioned arrays as demonstrated in the following example, which contains an expression:

```
>   LIMIT PRODUCT TO SCOTCH AND VODKA
>   LIMIT MONTH TO FEB AND MARCH
>   CREATE FORECAST FROM QUARTER*3
>   DISPLAY FORECAST
    PRODUCT        MONTH        FORECAST
    SCOTCH         FEB              16659
                   MAR              15411
    VODKA          FEB              24534
                   MAR              20712
```

In this case, the expressions QUARTER*3 is calculated only for selected elements and the dimensions of the new array named FORECAST are derived from the specified limits. In many cases, expressions will be used to combine distinct arrays in a mathematical sense as long as their dimensions are compatible.

Aggregation is defined as the process of "totaling" data so that the number of values is reduced in a meaningful way. With files, aggregation is applied with a key field, such as product or order number, so that target values are added up. With arrays, aggregation is applied across a dimension, thereby reducing the dimension of an array. The effect of an aggregation can by achieved through the DISPLAY command and a STORE command. The following command, for example, aggregates data by row (i.e., product) for two-dimensional array QUARTER:

```
>   DISPLAY QUARTER BY PRODUCT
    PRODUCT     QUARTER

    BOURBON       12936
    GIN           20540
    SCOTCH        15201
    VODKA         22786
```

or by column (i.e. month) with a grand total:

```
>   DISPLAY TOTAL QUARTER BY MONTH
    MONTH       QUARTER

    JAN           24294
    FEB           24305
    MAR           22864

    TOTAL         71463
```

The concept of aggregation through the DISPLAY command applies to arrays with other dimensions in a similar manner.

Aggregation through the STORE command achieves the same purposes as the previous examples, but saves the result for subsequent operations. The following statements create new arrays with reduced dimensions:

```
> STORE PRODSUM FROM QUARTER BY PRODUCT
> DISPLAY PRODSUM
  PRODUCT      PRODSUM

  BOURBON        12936
  GIN            20540
  SCOTCH         15201
  VODKA          22786


> STORE MONSUM FROM QUARTER BY MONTH
> DISPLAY TOTAL MONSUM
  MONTH        MONSUM

  JAN            24294
  FEB            24305
  MAR            22864

  TOTAL          71463
```

In most management support systems, there are additional facilities for performing aggregation, and the above presentation gives only a glimpse of representative facilities. For example, it is customary to combine selection and aggregation facilities as follows:

```
> LIMIT PRODUCT TO BOURBON AND SCOTCH
> STORE DARKPROD FROM QUARTER BY PRODUCT
> DISPLAY TOTAL DARKPROD
  PRODUCT      DARKPROD

  BOURBON        12936
  SCOTCH         15201

  TOTAL          28137
```

Many systems also incorporate features such as mathematical function, storage of expressions, spreadsheet analysis, and so forth. In addition, many of the above facilities, such as consolidation, selection, creation of new files and arrays, and aggregation, are available throughout database management software.

Natural Language Interface

Computer languages, such as the generic support language used above, various command and programming languages, and database languages, constitute the class of artificial languages created solely for the purpose of communicating with the computer. The notion of a natural language interface with the computer is right around the corner. In fact, several systems are presently in existence in artificial intelligence research laboratories. More attention will be given to this important topic for management support systems when the current emphasis on computational facilities diminishes.

RELATIONAL DATABASE MANAGEMENT

A *database* was defined earlier as a centralized collection of data stored for one or more computer applications. But there is more to it than that. One of the primary advantages of database technology is the factoring out of redundant data from an enterprise's data store. Thus, when file updates are required, only one copy need be changed. This subject generally has relevance for management support systems since it is conceivable that various activities can spawn several copies of the same data.

Representation

A *relational database management system* is based on a data model that is completely independent of how data is stored and accessed. Data is conceptually organized as an entity/attribute matrix (see Figure 3.10), and operational considerations are left completely to the database software. This is commonly regarded as a conceptual model of data.

A relational data view is similar in concept to the generic data structures presented in the preceding section. Data files and array data, as presented, represent the relational data view. Moreover, the file and array operations effectively reflect relational data operations.

Data Mapping

It is useful to recognize what the process of recording information involves. It is a relationship between members of two sets — hence

Attributes

	A_1	A_2	$\cdots$	A_n
E_1	$V_{1,1}$	$V_{1,2}$	$\cdots$	$V_{1,n}$
E_2	$V_{2,1}$	$V_{2,2}$	$\cdots$	$V_{2,n}$
Entities	.	.	(Values)	.
	.	.		.
	.	.		.
E_m	$V_{m,1}$	$V_{m,2}$	$\cdots$	$V_{m,n}$

Figure 3.10 Data representation can be conceptualized as an entity/attribute matrix.

the name *relational database*. Consider, for example, the ORDER file contained in Figure 3.4 and the sets *product code* and *order number*, depicted as follows:

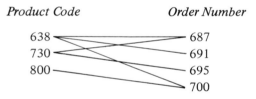

This is called a *data mapping*. It means that the product with code number 638 is included in orders 687, 691, and 700; order numbered 687 contains products numbered 638 and 730; and so forth.

If E is an identify attribute and V is an attribute set of the kinds mentioned above, then a *mapping* is denoted by:

$$\text{Mapping: } E \rightarrow V$$

Mappings are further classified as simple or complex. In a *simple mapping*, each element of E can be related to no more than one element of V. In a *complex mapping*, an element of E can be related to many elements of V. Moreover, if V is also an identity attribute set, then an *inverse mapping* is defined and denoted by:

$$\text{Inverse: } E \leftarrow V$$

For example, the product code and order number mapping, given previously, is a complex mapping in both directions.

The following combinations of simple and complex mappings are identified:

Mapping	Inverse Mapping
1. Simple	Simple
2. Simple	Complex
3. Complex	Simple
4. Complex	Complex

An example of case 1 is:

$$\text{Employee } \# \twoheadrightarrow \text{Social insurance } \#$$

where each employee has a unique social insurance number. An example of case 2 is:

$$\text{Insurance policy } \# \twoheadrightarrow \text{Billing date}$$

Because each insurance policy is billed on only one date, but on that date, many policies are billed. An example of case 3 is:

$$\text{School } \# \twoheadrightarrow \text{Student } \# \text{ (of students in school)}$$

because a school contains many students, but a student attends only one school. Finally an example of case 4 is:

$$\text{Part } \# \twoheadrightarrow \text{Warehouse } \# \text{ (of where parts are stored)}$$

because a particular kind of part is stored in many warehouses and each warehouse contains many parts.

Effective use of data mapping reduces or eliminates the redundancy in a database. Instead of storing an attribute for each identifier, only one copy of a unique attribute value is stored and the database is organized so that several identifiers can be related to it.

Figure 3.11 gives a relational view of two data mappings, represented symbolically as:

Department → Employee
Project → Employee

The identifiers are Dept #, Proj #, and Employee #. Clearly, the only data redundancy is inherent in the identifiers, and all department, project, and employee data are uniquely stored. (In actual practice, additional data would be stored for each entity.)

DEPARTMENT Relation		
Dept #	Manager	Location
1	Smith	New York
2	Jones	Chicago
3	Tnom	Los Angeles
4	Owens	Houston

PROJECT Relation		
Proj #	Name	Date
1	DB	1982
2	OS	1983
3	DSS	1984

EMPLOYEE Relation			
Dept #	Proj #	Employee #	Name
1	1	1	Hart
1	2	2	Alberts
2	3	3	Walters
2	1	4	Short
2	2	5	Jackson
3	3	6	Williams
3	1	7	Stone
4	2	8	Johns
4	1	9	Wright
4	3	10	Richards

Figure 3.11 Relational data view of two data nappings of the form Department → Employee and Project → Employee.

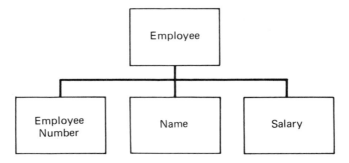

Figure 3.12 Example of a simple group.

Groups

In database terminology, a *group* is a set of data items and other groups. A group is *simple* if it contains only data items. A group is *compound* if it contains at least one other group – referred to informally as a subgroup. Figure 3.12 gives a schematic representation of a simple group and Figure 3.13 gives a schematic representation of a compound group.

In relational database theory, a relation does not contain "subgroups"; in other words, it is a simple group. In Figure 3.11, for

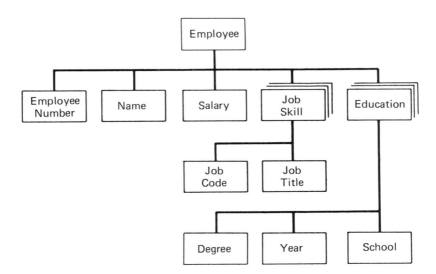

Figure 3.13 Example of a compound group.

example, it can be observed that all of the relations — DEPARTMENT, PROJECT, and EMPLOYEE — are simple groups.

Characteristics

An entity/attribute matrix in a relational database has the following properties:

1. Each row of the matrix represents an instance of the relation. A row is called a *tuple* in relational database theory.
2. The columns are homogeneous in the sense that all entries in a selected column are of the same data type. A column represents an attribute and is called a *domain*.
3. Each row of the matrix is unique as far as the identifier attribute is concerned, and the ordering is not significant.
4. Each column of the matrix represents an attribute, and the ordering of columns is not important.

An entity/attribute matrix that possesses these characteristics is referred to as *normalized*.

Relational database operations are defined on "normalized" relations. One aspect of dealing with relational database systems is the removal of "repeating groups" and compound groups through a process called *normalization*.

Normalization

The process of *normalization* involves eliminating the dependencies of a compound group or repeating groups without a loss of information. A *repeating group* is a multiple instance of a "subgroup," such as a list of dependents or several educational items.

The compound group in Figure 3.13 is used as an example to demonstrate normalization. It is represented symbolically as:

EMPLOYEE (*employee-number,* name, salary, job-skill, education)
JOB-SKILL (*job-code,* job-title)
EDUCATION (*degree,* year, school)

Clearly, this set of relations is not normalized.

E. F. Codd, the originator of the relational concept, gives the normalization procedure as follows:

Starting with the relation at the top of the tree [i.e., the tree corresponding to the compound group], take its primary key and expand each of the immediately subordinate relations by inserting this primary key domain [i.e., attribute value] or domain combination. The primary key of each expanded relation consists of the primary key before expansion augmented by the primary key copied down from the parent relation. Now, strike out from the parent relation all nonsimple domains [i.e., subordinate groups], remove the top node of the tree, and repeat the same sequence of operation on each remaining subtree.*

Figure 3.14 gives an instance of the application of this procedure to the compound group give in Figure 3.13. Symbolically, it can now be represented as:

EMPLOYEE (*employee-number,* name, salary)
JOB-SKILL (*employee-number, job-code,* job-title)
EDUCATION (*employee-number, degree,* year, school)

The multiple keys reflect the normalization procedure. Figure 3.15 gives an instance of the unnormalized and normalized relations given in this section.

The above form is known as the *first normal form.* Second and third normal forms are also defined for relational database models but are not within the scope of management support systems. The reader is referred to Codd's paper for additional information on this subject.

As a final example of normalization, Figure 3.16 gives the normalized form of the order file in Figure 3.4.

Operations

Relational database operations vary in scope and complexity based on the language features available to the designers of the database

---

*Codd, E. F., "A Relational Model of Data for Large Shared Data Banks," *Communications of the ACM,* Volume 13, Number 6, (June, 1970), p. 381.

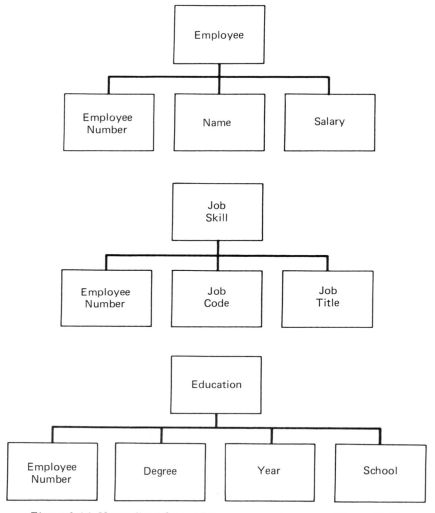

Figure 3.14 Normalized form of the compound group of Figure 3.13.

system. Facilities range from stand-alone database facilities to systems that allow interfacing from assemblers and higher-level language programs. Three operations are common to all relational systems:

- *Selection*
  This operation allows one or more tuples to be selected from a relation.

EMPLOYEE (employee-number	name	salary	JOB-SKILL (job-code	job-title)	EDUCATION (degree	year	school))
449795	JOHN A. DOE	44950.00	A23	Staff Exec.	BS	1950	M.I.T.
			F34	Mathematician	MBA	1955	Harvard
			G15	Actuary			
670042	L. K. SMITH	33619.50	L70	Personnel Man.	BBA	1950	Ohio
716832	S. BROWN	19500.00	F57	Systems Analyst	BS	1965	NYU
					MS	1967	NYU

Unnormalized Form

EMPLOYEE (employee-number | name | salary)
449795	JOHN A. DOE	44950.00
670043	L. K. SMITH	33619.50
716832	S. BROWN	19500.00

JOB-SKILL (employee-number | job-code | job-title)
449795	A23	Staff Exec.
449795	F34	Mathematician
449795	G15	Actuary
670043	L70	Personnel Man.
716832	F57	Systems Analyst

EDUCATION (employee-number | degree | year | school)
449795	BS	1950	M.I.T.
449795	MBA	1955	Harvard
670043	BBA	1950	Ohio
716832	BS	1965	NYU
716832	MS	1967	NYU

Normalized Form

Figure 3.15 An instance of the application of the normalization procedure.

PRODUCT Relation	
Product Code	Product Name
638	VALVE
730	PIN
800	PLATE

ORDER Relation			
Product Code	Order Number	Quantity	Dollars
638	687	5	150
638	691	10	250
638	700	15	300
730	687	100	500
730	695	500	2000
800	700	2	100

CUSTOMER Relation		
Order Number	Customer Number	Date
687	121	821015
691	320	821020
695	733	821028
700	528	821128

Figure 3.16 Normalized form of the order file in Figure 3.4.

- *Projection*
  This operation allows one or more domains to be selected from a relation.
- *Join*
  This operation allows two or more relations to be joined as though they existed as one relation.

Through judicious application of selection and projection operations, a particular attribute value can be isolated in a relation. The join operation allows relations in normalized form to combine for effective report generation.

SUMMARY

We are overloaded with information but are notably inept at using it effectively. Information surrounds us in many forms and we can evaluate it on the basis of its quantity and quality. Traditional EDP/MIS systems are reasonably good at handling preplanned transactions and reports but do not provide good management support. In order to fully support the decision maker, software and hardware facilities are needed for the accessible storage and reference of data.

The systems approach to information management recognizes and distinction between real, conceptual, and abstract systems and applies the concepts to the management support and database environment.

A *database* is a centralized collection of data stored for one or more computer applications. This concept involves the recognition of the enterprise, entities, entity sets, attributes, and information space. Through the use of software facilities, a database management system (DBMS) permits a subset of the abstract information space to be stored for access by a database command language (DBCL) and for management through a database description language (DBDL).

Because of the generality of management support systems, a collection of generic data structures, file operations, and array operations can be identified. *Generic data structures* include records, files, scalars, and array — all accessible by support software. *Generic file operations* include consolidation, selection, creation, aggregation, and a variety of computational operations and output functions. *Generic array operations* include selection, computational operations, creation, aggregation, and output functions. In the future, attention will be directed to a natural language interface to management support systems.

A *relational database management system* is a conceptual model based on entity/attribute matrices. Through a concept termed *data mapping*, redundant data is effectively factored out of an enterprise's data store. Data mapping can be simple or complex and can assume standard or inverse forms. A *group* is a set of data items and other groups. If a group contains only data items, it is called a *simple group*. If a group also contains subgroups, it is termed a *compound group*. In relational database theory, a relation is a simple group.

The process of *normalization* involves eliminating the dependencies of a compound group or repeating groups without a loss of information. A *repeating group* is a multiple instance of a "subgroup," such as a list of dependents. Procedures for normalization and several examples are presented. Common relational database operations are *selection, projection,* and *join.*

SELECTED READING

Atre, S., *Data Base: Structured Techniques for Design. Performance and Management*, New York: John Wiley & Sons, 1980.

Chamberlain, R. B., "The Promise — and Problems — Of Relational Data Base Design," *Computerworld* (In Depth), n.d., pp. 17–21.

Codd, E. F., "A Relational Model of Data for Large Shared Data Banks," *Communications of the ACM*, Volume 13, Number 6 (June, 1970), p. 381.

EXPRESS INTRODUCTORY MANUAL, Waltham, Massachusetts: Management Decision Systems, Inc., June 1981.

Hall, A. D., *A Methodology for Systems Engineering*, New York: Van Nostrand Reinhold Company, 1962.

Katzan, H., *Computer Data Management and Data Base Technology*, New York, Van Nostrand Reinhold Company, 1975.

Katzan, H., *Invitation to Pascal*, Princeton: Petrocelli Books, Inc., 1981.

Robinson, S. L., "Relational Data Bases: What? When? Where? Why?" *Computerworld* (In Depth), n.d., pp. 13–16.

SQL/Data System: Concepts and Facilities, Endicott, New York: IBM Corporation, Form #GH24-5013, 1982.

SQL/Data System: General Information, Endicott, New York: IBM Corporation, Form #GH24-5012, 1982.

Vetter, M., and Maddison, R. N., *Database Design Methodology*, Englewood Cliffs, New Jersey: Prentice/Hall International, 1981.

4
Providing Management
Support Services

INTRODUCTION

There are three important aspects of providing management support in a computer environment:

- Moving data into a position for access by a management support system
- Providing the proper organizational environment so end users can avail themselves of informational services
- Providing appropriate computer facilities to enhance management support

The first item was covered previously through six generic classifications: (1) files to database, (2) database to derived databases, (3) external databases, (4) time-sharing service, (5) down loading to microsystems, and (6) stand-alone microsystems. These classes can be arranged differently in order to establish an overall structure for providing management support:

a. External computer service
b. Internal computer service
c. Dedicated management support computers
   1. Medium- to large-scale computer support
   2. Stand-alone microsystems

Classes a, b, and c.1 have the common feature that they all require direct organizational support — not only in the area of planning and budgetary development but also with the objective of providing a central resource of everyday assistance, education, consulting, computer availability, and so forth. The *information center concept* is established to provide the latter services. Perhaps the same needs additionally apply to users of stand-alone microsystems.

The task of providing appropriate computer facilities to enhance management support is a key issue, since it involves computer hardware and software programs. The following sections provide a means of supplying this support.

INFORMATION CENTER CONCEPT

An *information center* is a group within an enterprise formed to facilitate end-user participation in the following activities:

- Application program development
- Access to enterprise databases
- Data planning for the enterprise
- Development of system prototypes

The information center concept is an alternative to traditional application development because it fosters end-user development rather than data processing development. In some instances, the information center (IC) will be organized within the data processing department and its manager will report directly to the top data processing manager. In other cases, an information center will be established in a headquarters or central location to provide a high level of user assistance without being unduly encumbered by data processing policies and procedures. The information center staff for the most part will be people with computer experience and knowledge of how the enterprise operates.

Operational Environment

The operational environment for an effective information center exists in an enterprise with EDP/MIS and management support systems needs that are somewhat characteristic of Figure 4.1. The informational requirements in this environment are varied. The *volume of information* involved may be a few fields from many records or it may be most or all fields from a few records. The *consistency of requirements* also varies. The same files may be used repeatedly in some cases and the needs may not even be predictable

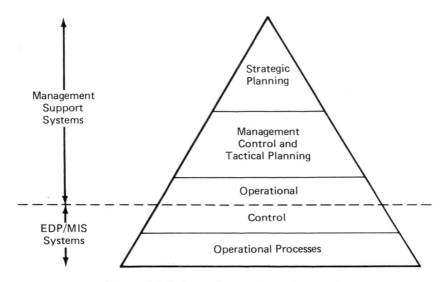

Figure 4.1 Information center environment.

in others. *Currency of data* can also be problematical to the system designer. Some end users may desire historical information, whereas others may require current operational information. Lastly, *usage patterns* may vary from frequent use as an integral part of one's job or it may be occasional and usually requested on a demand basis.

While these requirements certainly impact the needed hardware and software facilities available to information center users, they also determine its organization, its training, and its facilities.

Objectives

Based on the operational environment, it is evident that the information center will provide services to the end users that are not offered by the EDP/MIS department. As a group, the information center will select the appropriate end-user tools, manage data bases, and provide access to those data bases. Effectively, then, the *objective* of the information center is to supply the client population with productivity assistance that enhances access to the organization's informational resource and increases the self-sufficiency of the user in a computer environment.

Reasons for an Information Center

The motivation for the formation of an information center is largely the result of both increased needs on the part of the user and a decrease in the capability of the EDP/MIS department to satisfy these and other needs. In short, there is a backlog of applications to be developed in most EDP/MIS shops and an increase in requirements for services that are not satisfied by conventional transaction and report processing. The demonstrable evidence that supports the need for an information center is an increase in the use of outside time-sharing services, an increase in programming costs, and in some cases a decrease in the number of new applications entering the backlog queue. Thus, it would appear as though some users, at least, have given up.

Activities

User support activities can be direct or indirect. *Direct activities* are user education, consulting, and direct assistance. The last category necessarily includes a user help desk and a "hot line" for debugging assistance. *Consulting* is important for assisting the user in the selection of proper hardware and software tools and to insure that an end user is heading in the right direction. *Education* is an ongoing activity to acquaint new users with information center services and to update older users to new developments.

Indirect activities involve the management of computer and informational resources and of the information center itself. Continuous activities in this area include hardware and software evaluation, security, data base administration, technical development, planning, and other administrative and managerial tasks. In some organizations, promotion of the information center concept is necessary because of a historical dependence on centralized EDP/MIS service and for other geographical and organizational reasons. Figure 4.2 gives an overview diagram of information center operation.

An interface is necessary between the information center and the data processing center for two major reasons:

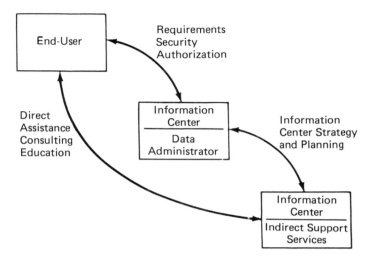

Figure 4.2 User interface with the information center.

- For adequate end-user support in the case that EDP/MIS resources are used
- For the coordination of the down loading of files and derived databases for end-user access when centralized facilities are not used

The information center concept is also beneficial to the EDP/MIS department, even though it may not seem that way on the surface. With an information center, highly trained computer personnel are better utilized while the effective service to the end-user community is improved. The application programming backlog is reduced, as is the need for application program maintenance.

Organization

The information center organization can report to the top EDP/MIS managers or exist as an independent unit, as covered above. Figure 4.3 gives a simple organization chart for an information center group. When the information center organization does not in fact report to the EDP/MIS department, then careful planning is required

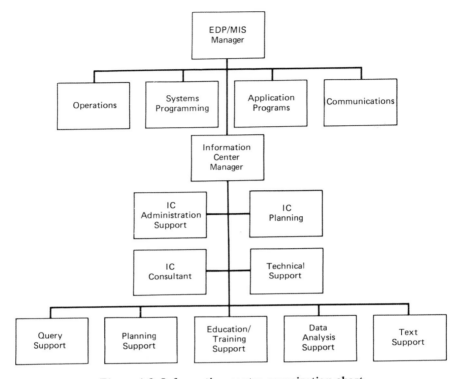

Figure 4.3 Information center organization chart.

to help insure that activities are appropriate to the fostering group. The EDP/MIS department should have influence over the operation of the information center.

Implementation

In order to assure success of the information center, a five-phase implementation plan is proposes.* The five phases are:

- Planning
- Start-up

---

*Squire, E., and Youstra, R., *Information Center Implementation Guide,* Washington: IBM Corporation, Form #GG22-9267, 1982.

- Pilot
- Expansion
- Continuing operation

Planning involves establishing a mission, identifying user requirements, selecting a pilot site, defining organizational structure and staff requirements, specifying hardware and software facilities, and so forth. *Start-up* provides the facilities to sustain information center operation and includes the development of job descriptions, selection of staff, establishment of office space, installation of hardware, development of procedures, and beginning of the pilot operation. The *pilot* tests the information center concept for an organization and helps to evaluate and refine user services. During this phase, user aids, documentation, and training materials, as well as administrative procedures, are developed. *Expansion* incorporates the opening of the Information Center with promotion, planning, charge and accounting, and the addition of new users. Finally, *continuing operation* is the ongoing process of evaluation, installation, education, and the analysis of "derived" user benefits.

War Room Concept

One concept that has been discussed recently is the "war room" concept whereby the physical facilities of an information center are equipped with output display devices, video telecommunications equipment, special input devices, and other managerial tools that permit the status of an enterprise to be displayed at any point in time. With the physical facilities located in a headquarters area, an executive can simply walk in and obtain needed information as a video display, a graphic output presentation, or a printed report. The information center is also used in some cases for the preparation of graphs, charts, slides, and transparencies for management presentation.

Postscript

The information center concept is a good idea. The biggest problem with it is determining an overall direction specifying what facilities and capabilities are needed. This requires a task force to concentrate on the issue. The biggest relief is the fact that the needed hardware and software can be purchased "off the shelf."

SUPPORT SYSTEM ARCHITECTURE

Sprague and Carlson use an interesting approach to the development of decision support systems.* They establish three primary technological components:

- A dialog manager
- A database manager
- A model manager

and then identify four DSS architectures based on systems comprised from combinations of these components.

The four DSS architectures presented by Sprague and Carlson are:

- DSS network
- DSS bridge
- DSS sandwich
- DSS tower

Each structure is briefly presented.

The *DSS network* (Figure 4.4) allows each component to interact with other components through a component interface manager and through component interfaces. The basic objective is to permit mixed components to interact — possibly developed by different groups at different times. This architecture allows component sharing and is inherently flexible. The connections are complicated, however, because of the diverse nature of interacting components.

The *DSS bridge* (see Figure 4.5) simplifies the interface between components by establishing a unified bridge component. In order to connect to other components, a component must adhere to the bridge's protocols. Local components are not accessible to other users, but shared components are available to all users. The use of shared components, such as a database, facilitates maintenance and component integration.

The *DSS sandwich* (see Figure 4.6) provides single dialog and database components, but allows different modeling components

---

*Sprague, R. W., Jr., and Carlson, E. D., *Building Effective Decision Support Systems*, Englewood Cliffs, New Jersey: Prentice-Hall, Inc., 1982.

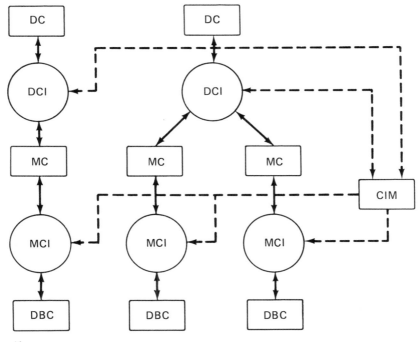

Key:
DC   — Dialog Component
MC   — Modeling Component
DBC   — Data Base Component
DCI   — Dialog Component Interface
MCI   — Modeling Component Interface
CIM   — Component Interface Manager

Figure 4.4 Sprague and Carlson's DSS network architecture.

When a modeling component is developed, it must be designed to interface with the dialog front end and the database back end. The advantage of this architecture is that separate modeling components can be integrated into a single system structure. The user need learn only one system and a centralized database can be accessed.

The final DSS architecture if the *DSS tower* (see Figure 4.7), which provides a means of connecting different hardware devices and database systems. The user need only learn one DSS system and may have a single "view" of the data — possibly through a relational database or a relational database front end to a network or hierarchical database system.

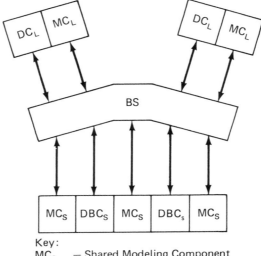

Key:
MC_S — Shared Modeling Component
DBC_S — Shared Data Base Component
DC_L — Local Dialog Component
MC_L — Local Modeling Component
BC — Bridge Component

Figure 4.5 Sprague and Carlson's DSS bridge architecture.

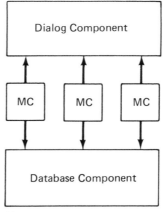

Key:
MC — Modeling Component

Figure 4.6 Sprague and Carlson's DSS sandwich architecture.

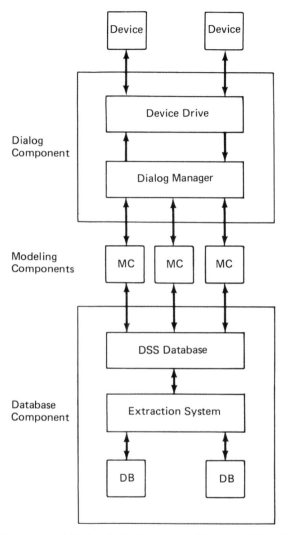

Figure 4.7 Sprague and Carlson's DSS tower architecture (slightly modified).

Clearly, DSS architecture is not a major consideration when a single dialog component interfaces with a single modeling component which interfaces with a single database component. When additional components are added, however, then overall structure does become a major issue, a case of "Pay me now or pay me later!"

INTEGRATED SUPPORT SYSTEM – A CASE STUDY

One of the fundamental problems with the design and implementation of management support systems is the obvious fact that most modern organizations already have computers installed and are providing a certain level of management support. Databases, query languages, and application programs and packages are in widespread use. Through the use of files-to-database and database-to-derived-database techniques, stand-alone support systems can be structured for effective results. In many other cases, however, management support systems must be integrated into an existing operational environment. Recently, The Sperry Corporation has announced an integrated decision support and development system. It is adopted here as a case study.

Overall Structure

The overall structure of Sperry's Decision Support and Development System is shown in Figure 4.8. This is an example of the DSS tower architecture presented in the preceding section. A single database view is permitted, and the user can interface with "modeling components" through a standard interactive language. The components are summarized as follows:

IPF (IPF 1100) – A dialog management system

QLP (QLP 1100) – A query language processor for database interaction

MAPPER (MAPPER 1100) – A general-purpose real-time report processing system

UCS (UCS 1100) – A universal compiling system

ADVISE (ADVISE 1100) – An information service that provides higher-level application development and conversational query capability

UDS (UDS 1100) – A universal data management system that permits different database systems to be accessed

Applications and file structures are standard. The key component is UDS 1100, which provides common access to relational and network/hierarchical databases and conventional data files.

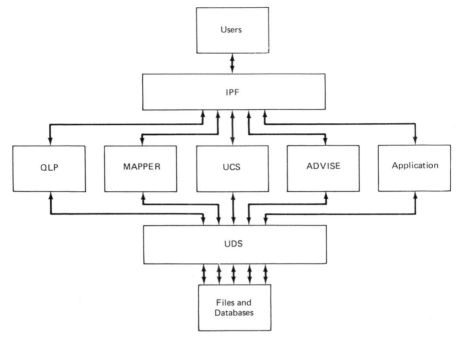

Figure 4.8 Overview diagram of Sperry's Decision Support and Development System.

Information Management

In a DSS tower architecture, a modeling component such as ADVISE 1100 must interface with the dialog and database component, as well as to other software and informational resources. Figure 4.9 gives a diagram of data access and control through ADVISE 1100.

Two new components are identified: a display processing system (DPS 1100) and a data dictionary system (DDS 1100). The *display processing system* is a software product for screen control and management, and the *data dictionary system* provides a means for the centralized description, location, and control of various data elements within a user database environment.

The information management system (ADVISE 1100 in this case) is, in a real sense, the management support system. It interacts with the user and database through preplanned interfaces, but essentially handles all queries, reports, display, and other processing functions as

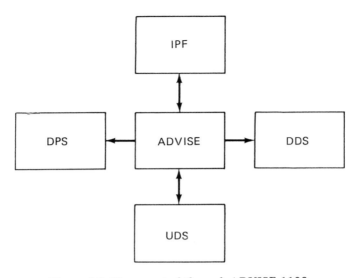

Figure 4.9 Flow control through ADVISE 1100

described previously under decision support, office information, and composite information systems.

Database Component

The database component (UDS 1100 in this case) — see Figure 4.10 — provides the translation of a relational user view of data to network/ hierarchical databases, relational databases, or files. Although the software at this level is indeed sophisticated, it is performed by a database administrator with a "relational translation language." Another important feature of the database component is a relational data manipulation language (RDML), which provides capability for executing the relational database operations introduced previously. Thus, we are effectively dealing here with layered software as one component is built on top of another.

Conclusion

Sperry's Decision Support and Development System is a complex and ambitious undertaking, but it will provide the high level of management support needed in a modern world. The single fact that it is totally integrated with systems software — such as the

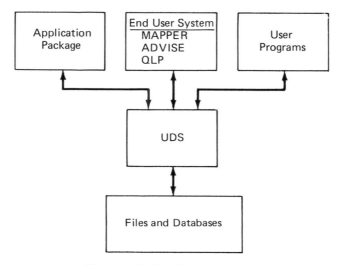

Figure 4.10 Database component.

operating system — is unique and gives some indication of future directions in this business.

SUMMARY

There are three important aspects of providing management support in a computer environment:

- Moving data into a position for access by a management support system
- Providing the proper organizational environment so end users can avail themselves of information services
- Providing appropriate computer facilities to enhance management support

The first item involves the data transfer methods — such as "files to database" — covered earlier. The second and third items can be achieved through an information center and an integrated support system.

An information center is a group within an enterprise formed to facilitate end-user participation in the following activities:

* Application program development
* Access to enterprise databases
* Data planning for the enterprise
* Development of systems prototypes

The information center concept is an alternative to traditional application development because it fosters end-user development. While the informational and computational needs of an end-user population are varied, it is clear that an information center will provide services to the end users that are not offered by the EDP/MIS department. Much of the motivation for an information center stems from increased user needs and a lessening of the ability of the EDP/MIS department to satisfy them. An information center generally provides direct assistance, consulting, and education services to its user population. However, there are many behind-the-scene tasks that are normally performed on behalf of the organization. A five-phase implementation plan is proposed: planning, start-up, pilot, expansion, and continuing operation.

Support system architecture can be synthesized from three primary technological components: a dialog manager, a database manager, and a model manager. Based on these components, four DSS architectures are presented:

* DSS network
* DSS bridge
* DSS sandwich
* DSS tower

Each architecture has unique characteristics, as well as advantages and disadvantages.

A case study representing the DSS tower architecture is presented. It is Sperry's Decision Support and Development System that gives examples of a modeling component (ADVISE 1100), a database component (UDS 1100), and a dialog component (IPF 1100), as well as a variety of other management support software components.

SELECTED READING

Katzan, H., *Distributed Information Systems,* Princeton: Petrocelli Books, Inc., 1979.

Sperry Corporation publications:
- 1100 OS Facts and Figures, Form #U7077RI
- 1100 Series
  Decision Support and Development System, Form #U7238
- ADVISE 1100
  Advanced Information Services User's Description, Form #U7239
- ADVISE 1100
  Advanced Information Services
  Administrator's Description, Form #U7249
- UDS 1100
  Universal Data System User's Description, Form #U7240
- UDS 1100
  Universal Data System Administrator's Description, Form #U7250
- The MAPPER System: The Next Generation, Form #U7241
- The MAPPER 1100 System User Perspective, Form #U7191

Worldwide Communications, P.O. Box 500, Blue Bell, Pennsylvania, 1982.

Sprague, R. H., Jr., and Carlson, E. D., *Building Effective Decision Support Systems,* Englewood Cliffs, New Jersey: Prentice-Hall, Inc., 1982.

Squire, E., and Youstra, R., *Information Center Implementation Guide,* Washington, D.C.: IBM Corporation, Form #GG22-9267, 1982.

Yowell, C. E., *External Data Access in an Information Center Environment,* White Plains, New York: IBM Corporation, Form #G320-6358, 1980.

5
Strategic Planning for
Management Support Systems

INTRODUCTION

Management support systems are unique in that they combine a complex technology with a historically unstructured working environment. The complex technology is computers and the working environment is the management arena. The term *management support system* refers to the use of computer-based information systems to enhance executive, management, and administrative decision making through the use of decision support systems, reporting systems, office information systems, modeling/simulation/ optimization systems, and database systems.

Because diverse groups in a business enterprise are impacted by management support systems and the applications are complex, planning is particularly significant.

This section covers the key areas of strategic planning for management support systems, selection of projects, justification, and acceptance. Collectively, the information presented here can be used as a guideline to the development of a strategic plan for a management support system and subsequently an overall support system concept.

STRATEGY AND PLANNING

Because management support systems represent an evolving technology, the key question is not what should be done tomorrow, but rather what should be done today to prepare for an uncertain future. Thus, the dimensions of a management support strategy are threefold: direction and goals a framework for action, and a rationale for decision making. A strategy does not specify individual applications, provide justification, and give a definition of the inherent technology.

Contents of the Strategy

A management support strategy gives three things:

* Where we are (*current position*)
* Where we are going (*goals*)
* How we get there (*direction*)

The *current position* is a specification of the equipment, already installed applications, trained and knowledgeable people, and existing organizational problems that have a bearing on a management support plan. *Goals* are certainly dependent upon a particular enterprise but include factors such as better customer service, increased sales volume with the same head count, reduction of administrative expense, job enhancement, the establishment of new markets, and more timely and effective decision making.

The *direction* (or "How do we get there?") is a major issue – in fact, it is the reason for a strategy in the first place. Direction needs policies and procedures in the following areas:

* Justification
* Implementation
* User acceptance
* Staffing and organization

The above areas form the basis for a strategic plan that gives the stages of tactical (or functional planning) for the enterprise.

Strategic Plan

The strategic plan for a management support system covers three stages of work: preparatory work, development of a tactical plan, and utilization of the tactical plan.

The *preparatory work* is crucial because it sets the stage for success or failure. The history of planning in an enterprise should first be consulted because a management support strategy will eventually become part of a larger planning entity. A high-level management commitment – or sponsor – is needed to kick off an effective project. Responsibility for management support and also for tactical planning should be assigned and a strategy group should be formed. Participation in any of the above activities need not be on a full-time basis, but the key objective is to specify basic objectives and output of the strategy sessions.

The *sponsor* is particularly significant because resources have to be obtained for management support and even for planning itself, and the needed policies must be set and enforced.

In the *development of the plan,* assumptions must clearly be made concerning the organizational structure, the staff, and the relevant technology. After the gathering and analysis of information about the organization, a sequence of management support applications is selected. Objectives are required at this point and they must minimally include opportunities, goals that can be measured, time frames, and any problems that are anticipated. The strategic plan, at this point, should be reviewed with local management in the areas of data processing, communications, administration, facilities, and personnel and then be presented to top management.

In the *utilization of the plan,* approval is requested for initial activities that include pilot projects, research efforts, and associated development work. A means of using the plan is also needed, which includes people, procedures, and a user feedback channel. The plan should also include an action item to be updated in line with the planning policies of the enterprise.

Guidelines

In outlining a strategy and developing a plan for management support, a few pertinent guidelines are helpful for increasing the chance of project success. The most important consideration is to concentrate resources in time and in place and focus these resources on the stated objectives. Secondly, it is not prudent to allocate resources unless there is a better than average chance of success. There are simply too many intangibles in management support to insure immediate success, and user acceptance can be problematical unless handled properly. Naturally, due consideration of user acceptance is an important aspect of strategic planning. Lastly, it goes almost without saying that you should not compete for the organization's resources unless the conditions are favorable to the capacities of your organizational unit, and also you should not try to obtain these resources unless they will contribute to your organizational unit's strategic objectives.

JUSTIFICATION

Enthusiasm over management support is contagious. The technology of relational database management, for example, is both exciting and interesting. It is likely that this enthusiasm will carry over to the executive suite, where seasoned executives will recognize the glamour over the newly discovered source of productivity. Moreover, justification will be required — regardless of the credibility and access of the sponsor.

Definition

Justification is the information presented to a decision maker to support an investment proposal. In general, there are two *major* reasons to provide justification:

1. To achieve agreement to put an investment proposal in an overall plan for the organization
2. To obtain a commitment of resources for an implementation project

In the area of management support, justification is notably difficult since hard money is being balanced against soft savings.

Methodology

Traditional methods of justification include almost any form of inductive reasoning. Some of the more noteworthy are:

- Cost of automation versus the manual method
- Improve customer service
- There is no other way to do it
- Gives a competitive advantage
- It is part of the cost of doing business
- It is our "image" to be at the leading edge

With management support, a useful approach is to depict a labor cost curve with a flattened slope achieved by increasing the efficiency and effectiveness of the affected personnel. This is productivity.

Productivity

Productivity is a key benefit of management support systems because it provides an increased quality and quantity of work, an increased span of control, more effective (i.e., more timely) work, and decreased turnover of key people. Thus, *productivity* can be more formally specified as the relationship between the output of a work environment to its input in labor and raw materials.

Methods of Analysis

Two methods of delineating productivity are the payback method and the cash flow method.

The *payback method* reflects costs that are displaced because of management support technology. Using videoconferencing as an example, travel costs are reduced through meetings and conferences conducted via the latest methods in video technology. Clearly, a certain percent of travel costs are replaced per year, and after a period of years, the initial investment in equipment pays for itself.

With the *cash flow method* of analysis, costs are not replaced by the newer technology but they are reduced. Ad hoc versus periodic reports serve as an example. As the level of ad hoc reporting increases, costs incurred because of a high level of planned reports decrease. Thus, reports are generated *only* when needed.

In some cases, therefore, labor, equipment, and facilities costs are displaced and *cost savings* result. Typical examples are: floor space for files, travel costs, postage costs, forms and supplies costs, and time savings. In other cases, *cost avoidance* takes place because there is decreased growth of staff, equipment, and facilities.

IMPLEMENTATION

The term *implementation* refers here to a pilot project to establish a concept and then an expansion both horizontally and vertically within the organization. In this context, horizontal expansion refers to a proliferation of the same application throughout the organization. Vertical expansion refers to an enhancement of the application domain to add new functionality.

The Pilot Project Approach

A pilot project is a forerunner of a larger project or application with the objective of building confidence in a new idea. A pilot project is a learning experience that demonstrates technical feasibility, costs, benefits, and user acceptance. Effectively, a "pilot" is a means of planning big and starting small.

Clearly, a pilot project is an approach to experiential learning and to gauging user resistance. Some approaches that have been taken are to give the management support functionality to some groups and not others or to give the functionality to all groups and then take it away from one of them. The objective in both cases is to measure productivity, take interviews, and give questionnaires to assess the success of the project.

In many cases, and particularly in the area of management support, people simply do not know what they want and do not know what they need. A pilot project is a means of determining valuable input to the planning process without spending an excessive amount of money. It is also a means of finding mistakes and problems early and thereby minimizing exposure. If a pilot project flops, it is chalked up to experience. If a heavily committed project fails, it is blamed on more serious factors.

Selecting a Climate for Success

The best pilot project is naturally one with a high probability of success. The object system should be easy to use and easy to learn. It should be assigned to a relatively small close-knit group with good internal communication, so they can aid one another, and an enthusiastic manager. Most importantly, a pilot project must not be placed in a pressure group that may not give a concept a fair evaluation.

The time duration for a pilot project must be long enough for the people to become accustomed to the system but short enough so the momentum and enthusiastic atmosphere do not subside. Most experts agree that two to six months is the optimum duration.

A group of users who are currently using terminals is a good candidate for a pilot system. It is also important that the people in the selected group recognize that they need improvement. While these factors are not always possible, it greatly increases the chances of success if they exist.

Choosing the Right Application

As long as management support systems are dependent upon people, it is necessary to involve people in the pilot project. If a person can achieve personal success with a system, that person will be the best source of support.

USER ACCEPTANCE

Management support systems are a change agent, so the success of a project is largely dependent upon the user's reaction to it. In the implementation phase, it is important that the people regard the system as their own. As a result, much of change management is dependent upon an acceptance strategy, resistance management, and proper education and training.

Acceptance Strategy

A successful acceptance strategy is anticipatory, so fears, resistance, and expectations must be identified early in the implementation plan. The announcement of the plan should be made early in the change cycle, and significant policy questions have to be addressed.

The system announcement should in general be made to the affected department by a high-level executive, giving the objectives, benefits to the individual and the organization, expectations, feedback mechanism, and user implementation schedule.

The acceptance strategy is a link between the strategic and tactical plans of an enterprise and covers personnel policies regarding relocation, associated job levels, training plans, and requirements for using the management support equipment.

Resistance Management

Some of the factors that contribute to a reduced resistance are also good management practices in general. Probably the most significant aspect to consider in this area is the human factors of the hardware, software, and work environment. Ample free "terminal" time is an absolute must, and no worker statistics should be collected. A "help" desk, already available in many data processing departments, is useful for easing tensions but also serves as a window into the functionality of the system.

Education and Training

The existence of training programs in modern organizations is presently taken for granted. It is supplied by practically all vendors and in-house training groups.

Best results are achieved when the subject matter is presented in the following sequence: overview, a basic functions course, an advanced functions course, and tutorials interspersed whenever necessary.

Training should be timed with the acquisition of functionality. If training is performed too early, the end users lose their enthusiasm and confidence, and the chances of user acceptance are lessened.

SUMMARY

Management support systems are unique because they combine a complex technology with a historically unstructured working environment. The complex technology is computers and the working environment is the management arena. Strategic planning is particularly signifiant because diverse groups in a business enterprise are impacted by management support systems, and the applications are complex.

The key question is not what should be done tomorrow, but rather what should be done today to prepare for an uncertain future. The dimensions of a management support strategy are threefold: direction and goals, a framework for action, and a rationale for decision making. A strategy for management support stresses the current position, goals, and direction.

The success of a strategic plan is dependent upon good preparatory work and a sponsor within the organization. Acceptance of a plan is dependent upon justification, which involves both agreement and also a commitment of resources. Methods of financial analysis include the payback method and the cash flow method.

The implementation of a strategic plan normally involves a pilot project followed by horizontal and vertical expansion within the organization. Significant factors include choosing the right application and insuring that there is a climate for success. User acceptance is directly related to resistance management and effective education and training.

SELECTED READING

Drucker, P. F., *Managing in Turbulent Times,* London: Pan Books, 1980.

McLean, E. R., and Soden, J. V., *Strategic Planning for MIS,* New York: John Wiley & Sons, 1977.

Steiner, G. A., *Strategic Planning: What Every Manager Should Know,* New York: The Free Press, 1979.

Bibliography

Alter, S., *Decision Support Systems: Current Practice and Continuing Challenges,* Reading, Massachusetts: Addison-Wesley Publishing Company, 1980.

Alter, S., "What Do You Need to Know to Develop Your Own DSS?" *DSS-82 Transactions,* San Francisco (June 14–16, 1982), pp. 109–115.

Atre, S., *Data Base: Structured Techniques for Design, Performance, and Management,* New York: John Wiley & Sons, 1980.

Barr, A., and Feigenbaum, E. A. (Editors), *The Handbook of Artificial Intelligence,* Volume 1, Los Altos, California: William Kaufmann, Inc., 1981.

Blanning, R. W., "The Functions of a Decision Support System," *Information and Management,* Volume 2, Number 3, pp. 87–93.

Chamberlain, R. B., "The Promise – and Problems – Of Relational Data Base Design," *Computerworld* (In depth), n.d., pp. 17–21.

Codd, E. F., "A relational model of data for large shared data banks," *Communications of the ACM,* Volume 13, Number 6 (June 1970), p. 381.

Cohen, C., *Composite Information Systems: Risk Factors and Implementation Strategies,* Arthur Anderson & Company, Presented at the DSS-82 Conference, San Francisco, 1982.

Drucker, P. F., *Managing in Turbulent Times,* London: Pan Books, 1980.

DSS Transactions (Gary W. Dickson, Editor), San Francisco (June 14–16, 1982).

EXPRESS Introductory Manual, Waltham, Massachusetts: Management Decision Systems, Inc., June, 1981.

Glaser, R., and Glaser, C., *Managing by Design,* Reading, Massachusetts: Addison-Wesley Publishing Company, 1981.

Hall, A. D., *A Methodology for Systems Engineering,* New York: Van Nostrand Reinhold Company, 1962.

Harvard Business Review, *On Human Relations,* New York: Harper & Row, Publishers, 1979.

Katzan, H., *Computer Data Management and Data Base Technology,* New York: Van Nostrand Reinhold Company, 1975.

Katzan, H., *Distributed Information Systems,* Princeton: Petrocelli Books, Inc., 1979.

Katzan, H., *Multinational Computer Systems: An Introduction to Transnational Data Flow and Data Regulation,* New York: Van Nostrand Reinhold Company, 1980.

Katzan, H., *Invitation to Pascal,* Princeton: Petrocelli Books, Inc., 1981.

Keen, P. G. W., and Morton, M. S. S., *Decision Support Systems: An Organizational Perspective,* Reading, Massachusetts: Addison-Wesley Publishing Company, 1978.

Luft, J., *Of Human Interaction,* Palo Alto, California: National Press Books, 1969.

Martin, J., *An End-User's Guide to Data Base,* Englewood Cliffs, New Jersey: Prentice-Hall, Inc., 1981.

McKenney, J. L., and Keen, P. G. W., "How Managers' Minds Work," Harvard Business Review, *On Human Relations,* New York: Harper & Row, 1979, pp. 30–47.

McLean, E. R., and Soden, J. V., *Strategic Planning for MIS,* New York: John Wiley & Sons, 1977.

Mintberg, H., "Planning on the Left Side and Managing on the Right," Harvard Business Review, *On Human Relations,* New York: Harper & Row, 1979, pp. 4–10.

Monypenney, R., "Person/Role Conflict in the DSS-Corporate Interface," *DSS-82 Transactions,* San Francisco (June 14–16, 1982), pp. 67–73.

Nolan, R. E., Young, R. T., and Di Sylvester, B. C., *Improving Productivity Through Advanced Office Controls,* New York: Amacom, 1980.

Robinson, S. L., "Relational Data Bases: What? When? Where? Why?" *Computerworld* (In depth), n.d., pp. 13–16.

Rockart, J. F., and Treacy, M. E., "The CEO goes on-line," *Harvard Business Review,* Volume 60, Number 1 (January–February, 1982), pp. 82–88.

Sowell, T., *Knowledge and Decisions,* New York: Basic Books, Inc., 1980.

Sperry Corporation publications:
- 1100 OS Facts and Figures, Form #U7077RI
- 1100 Series
  Decision Support and Development System, Form #U7238
- ADVISE 1100
  Advanced Information Services User's Description, Form #U7239
- ADVISE 1100
  Advanced Information Services Administrator's Description, Form #U7249
- UDS 1100
  Universal Data System User's Description, Form #U7240
- UDS 1100
  Universal Data System Administrator's Description, Form #U7250
- The MAPPER System: The Next Generation, Form #U7241
- The MAPPER 1100 System
  User Perspective, Form #U7191

Worldwide Communications, P.O. Box 500, Blue Bell, Pennsylvania, 1982.

Sprague, R. H., Jr., and Carlson, E. D., *Building Effective Decision Support Systems,* Englewood Cliffs, New Jersey: Prentice-Hall, Inc., 1982.

Squire, E., and Youstra, R., *Information Center Implementation Guide,* Washington: IBM Corporation, Form #GG22-9267, 1982.

SQL/Data System: Concepts and Facilities, Endicott, New York: IBM Corporation, Form #GH24-5013, 1982.

SQL/Data System: General Information, Endicott, New York: IBM Corporation, Form #GH24-5012, 1982.

Steiner, G. A., *Strategic Planning: What Every Manager Must Know*, New York: The Free Press, 1979.

Vetter, M., and Maddison, R. N., *Database Design Methodology*, Englewood Cliffs, New Jersey: Prentice-Hall International, 1981.

Yowell, C. O., *External Data Access in an Information Center Environment*, White Plains, New York: IBM Corporation, Form #G320-6358, 1980.

Index

Abstract system, 48
Acceptance strategy, 106
Access routines, 54
Ad hoc reports, 2
ADVISE 1100, 94, 95
Aggregation, 62, 63, 69
Alpha area, 4
Alter, Steven L., 12, 41, 42
Application database, 29
Array, 55
Array operations, 64
Array variables, 64
Arithmetic expressions, 67
Artificial intelligence research, 41
Attribute, 49
Attribute set, 50
Audio conferencing, 14

Banking case study, 21
Beta area, 5
Blanning, R.W., 28
Blind quadrant, 3

Carlson, E.D., 90
Cash flow method, 104
Choosing the right application, 106
Closed system, 48
Codd, E.F., 77
Cognitive style, 7, 9
Communicating word processors, 14
Complex mapping, 72
Composite, 14
Composite information system, 11, 14
Compound group, 75, 81
Computer-based information system, 1
Computer conferencing, 14
Conceptual model, 48
Conceptual system, 48
Conditional test, 67
Conferencing, 13
Consistency of requirements, 84
Consolidation, 60

Consulting, 86
Contents of the strategy 101
Continuing operation, 89
Corporate reporting system, 2, 14
Cost avoidance, 104
Cost savings result, 104
Creation, 60
CRS, *see* Corporate reporting system
Currency of data, 85
Current position, 101

Data administration, 20
Data analysis, 13
Database, 49, 52, 54, 71, 81
Database administrator, 54
Database command language, 53
Database description language, 53
Database manager, 53, 90
Database query, 37
Database to derived database, 29
Data dictionary system, 95
Data file, 55
Data mapping, 71, 72, 81
Data retrieval, 13
DBA, *see* Database administrator
DDS 1100, 95
Decision support system, 1, 2, 11, 12
Delta area, 5
Derived database, 29
Descriptor, 51
Design of a viable solution, 9
Development of the plan, 102
Diagnosis of a decision situation, 8
Dialog manager, 90
Direct activities, 86
Direction, 101
DPS 1100, 95
Domain, 76
Down loading to microsystems, 33
DSS bridge, 90
DSS network, 90
DSS sandwich, 90

DSS, *see* Decision support system
DSS tower, 90

Editing function, 20
Education, 86
Education and training, 107
80-20 rule, 7, 35
Electronic mail system, 13
Entity, 47, 49
Entity set, 50
Environment, 48
Expansion, 89
EXPRESS system, 54
External database, 32
External data structures, 59
Extract program, 33

Field, 54
File, 55
File operations, 59
Files to database, 29
First normal form, 77
Forecasting, 38
Functionality, 27–28

Generic array operations, 81
Generic data structures, 81
Generic file operations, 81
Goals, 101
Group, 75, 81
Guidelines, 102

Hard information, 8
Hidden quadrant, 3
Homogeneous data, 55
Horizontal expansion, 104
Human resources case study, 16

IC, *see* Information center
Identifier, 50
Implementation, 104
Indirect activities, 86
Information center, 83, 84, 97
    activities, 86
    implementation, 88
    objective, 85
    organization, 87
    reasons for, 86
Information dynamics, 7
Information overload, 46

Information space, 3, 51
Integrated support system case study, 94
Internal data structures, 59
Intuitive manager, 8
Intuitive modality, 9
Inverse mapping, 72
IPF 1100, 94

Johari analysis, 4, 6
Johari model, 4
Johari theory, 3
Johari window, 3
Join, 80, 81
Justification, 103

Keen, P.G.W., 41
Knowledge-based systems, 40
Knowledge representation, 40

Leadership styles, 9
Left hemisphere of the brain, 8
Less formal methods, 8
Linear array, 55

Management information system, 2, 6
Management style, 25
Management support system, 2, 4, 25, 27, 100
Managerial judgment, 6
Managerial style, 7
MAPPER 1100, 94
Matrix, 55
Methods of analysis, 104
MIS, *see* Management information system
MMS, *see* Model management system
Model management system, 2
Model manager, 90
Monypenney, Richard, 36
Morton, M.S.S., 41
MSS, *see* Management support system

Natural form, 65
Natural language interface, 71
Normalization, 76, 81

Office information system, 2, 11, 13
OIS, *see* Office information system
Omega area, 6
Open quadrant, 3
Open system, 48

Operational data, 49
Operations, 20
Organizational environment, 27

Patterns of user interaction and data flow, 36
Payback method, 104
Periodic reports, 2
Pilot, 89
Pilot project approach, 105
Planning, 89
Preceptive modality, 8
Preparatory work, 101
Primary key, 50
Productivity, 1, 25, 104
Projection, 80, 81
Pseudo information processor, 7

QLP 1100, 94

RDML, *see* Relational data manipulation
   language
Real system, 48
Receptive modality, 8
Record, 55
Recorded information, 48
Relational database, 72
Relational database management, 71, 81
Relational data manipulation language, 96
Relational data view, 71
Relationship, 48
Repeating group, 76, 81
Resistance management, 106
Retrieval and analysis, 20
Right hemisphere of the brain, 8

Scalar, 55
Schema, 53
Selecting a climate for success, 105
Selection, 60, 65, 78, 81
Semistructured, 48
Semistructured decisions, 6
Simple group, 75, 81
Simple mapping, 72
Simulation, 13
Soft information, 8
Special purpose decision support, 39

Sperry Corporation's decision support
   system, 94
Sponsor, 102
Sprague, R.W., 90
Spreadsheet form, 65
Squire, E., 88
Standalone microsystems, 35
Start-up, 89
Strategic plan, 101
Strategy and planning, 100
Structured decision, 48
Structured decisions, 6
Subject database, 29
Subtotal function, 63
Support, 11
Support system architecture, 90, 98
Synchronous data communications facility,
   33
System, 47
Systematic manager, 8
Systematic methods, 8
Systematic modality, 9
Systems ontology, 47

Time sharing service, 32
Total function, 69
Tuple, 76

UCS 1100, 94
UDS 1100, 94, 96
Unknown area, 4
Unstructured decisions, 6, 7
Usage patterns, 85
User acceptance, 106
User view, 59
Utilitzation of the plan, 102

Variables, 64
Vertical expansion, 104
Video conferencing, 14
Volume of information, 84

War room concept, 89
What if analysis, 39
Word processing capability, 13

Youstra, R., 88